Dust
Bowl
Diary

*Ann
Marie
Low*

University of Nebraska Press *Lincoln and London*

The paper in this book meets
the guidelines for permanence
and durability of the Committee
on Production Guidelines for
Book Longevity of the Council
on Library Resources.

Library of Congress Cataloging
in Publication Data

Low, Ann Marie, 1912-
Dust bowl diary.

1. Low, Ann Marie, 1912-
2. North Dakota – Biography.
3. Farm Life – North Dakota –
History – 20th century.
4. North Dakota – Social
conditions.   5. North Dakota –
Economic conditions.
6. Depressions – 1929 –
United States.   I. Title.
F636.L92   1984
978.4'032'0924   84-3672
ISBN 0-8032-2864-3
(alk. paper)
ISBN 0-8032-7913-2
(pbk. : alk. paper)

Dedicated to

Bennie Woolley, Creative Writing Instructor at
Yavapai College, and to Bernice Brown and
Dorothy L. Murphy, freelance writers in Sedona,
Arizona, for their help and encouragement

Contents

Preface

"Talk about wind! Most of the scenery is in the air." These words hit my eyes as I opened my fifty-year-old diary that I found while rummaging in a trunk. The words brought it all back: the Dust Bowl years; the loss of the Stony Brook country—a loss still a heartache after all these years. My old diary tells the story of that period of history, and what it did to my family, from my point of view, that of a woman who lived it. Our family consisted of my father and mother, me, my younger sister, Ethel, and brother Bud, the youngest, living on a large stock farm in southeastern North Dakota. My father's mother and his two brothers, Grover and Ted, much younger than he, lived on the old family homestead two and a half miles away.

This book is based upon the diary I kept between 1927 and 1937. Much of it, of no interest beyond my immediate family, has been omitted. The only additions are a few details not included in my diary but written at that time in letters to my father's sister Evalyn. She kept some of my letters, which were returned to me after her death. I have added narrative material to fill in gaps in the story. When the diary and the narrative were put together, it became apparent that I had two stories to tell: the account of the effect of the drouth, depression, and government programs upon my family and neighbors, and the story of my own coming to maturity under frustrating family circumstances, hampered by the restrictions society at that time placed upon young women, and in the face of poverty, seeing all we had worked for slip away.

The place names are factual. Nearly all names of the people mentioned have been changed with the exception of mine, my husband's, and those of my parents, Mr. and Mrs. H. A. Riebe; the members of the Ferguson family; my father's brothers and sisters; and those three notable old-timers, Bill Follis, Archie McKecknie, and Ben Bird.

The Breeze

My diary starts in 1927, the last of the "good years" before the Great Depression. From 1900 until the 1920s there had been prosperity in North Dakota. Land worth about ten dollars an acre in 1900 was worth thirty-five dollars in 1920. After World War I, prices dropped and farmers were left in debt for expansion during the war and were faced with high taxes and high prices for goods they had to buy.

Dad hated and avoided debt. Through 1927 he continued to prosper. My diary records that when he came back from St. Paul that autumn after selling his cattle, he brought back expensive presents for his children and a sealskin coat and black silk dress for Mama. The diary also says, "I think a pink silk dress would be pretty on her, or a soft green to bring out the green in her eyes. Here all women past forty wear black dresses for best. When I get to be forty I'll wear a pink dress if I want to and never mind if the neighbors think I am trying to be young and frivolous."

Ethel and I were sophomores in high school that year and Bud was in the seventh grade. Previously we had attended a one-room rural school of all eight grades only a mile and a half from home. We walked to it or drove a horse and buggy or horse and sleigh. After I finished the eighth grade, Dad and Mama had me wait until Ethel finished and I was old enough to get a permit to drive a car. Then I drove Ethel, Bud, and myself to the town school seven miles away. When winter weather and roads prohibited driving, Dad hired a man named John to help do the farm work and his wife, Theresa, to keep house while Mama rented rooms in town and stayed there with us during the winter.

One day that fall, before we moved to town, I wrote in my diary,

Dad decided not to hire a man for shocking this year, so he and Bud and I shocked all the grain. With Bud and me in school, he has had to hire a man for fall plowing, a young fellow named Bill from Oklahoma he found bumming around town. Bill came up for harvest work, lost all his money in a crap game, and needs to earn some to get home. He is not much good with horses but is crazy to ride my Pronto. I won't let him. She was abused by a man before I got her. With time and patience I taught her to trust me. To this day, when a man goes near her, she tries to kick him into Kingdom Come.

Today I heard a commotion in the barn and rushed out to see what was going on. Pronto was standing in her stall looking half asleep. Bill was lying on the other side of the barn beneath my saddle and saddle blanket, looking as surprised as a dog with his first porcupine.

"Bill! What have you done?"

"What have I done? That's what I hate about two-facedness. To look at that horse you'd think I did all this myself."

Tonight, after the chores were done, I rode Pronto out into the hills. How I love these hills, especially at sunset!

CHAPTER I

The Hail Storm

By April of 1928 the roads were passable enough for Mama, Bud, Ethel, and me to get home from town on weekends.

April 30, 1928
Saturday we baked, washed, ironed, scrubbed floors, churned, and painted the kitchen. In the late afternoon I rode to the lake to see Grover, who was seeding his land up there, went one round with him, and then had to come home to milk cows. The thought now filters into my dim brain that I should never have learned to milk. Mama and Ethel never did.

Mama, unlike most farm women, never learned to milk and did very little outside work. Neither did Ethel. When she was eight years old the local doctor told Dad and Mama she had a heart murmur. Dad and Mama, frightened lest they lose Ethel, took very good care of her. Long before 1928 it was obvious that Ethel was physically capable of almost anything she wanted to do, but by that time the pattern in our family was set.

For a number of years, before we needed cream to sell, all we had was one family milk cow. The men hated to milk cows. When Bud was about nine years old, and I about twelve, a hired man taught us to milk. We had no dairy cows then and just milked a few range cows who gave more milk than the average range cow.

They could run like deer and kick a cat off a fence post without touching the post. Rounding up those cows twice a day and getting them milked furnished all the excitement and adventure our young souls craved. By 1928 the cows were tamer and furnished less of our entertainment, but most of our amusements still had to be free.

Grover told me that once when he and his hired man, Willie, were getting a load of hay, Willie killed twenty mice at the stack and took them home to feed the cats. He fed them several that evening and put the rest in a bucket to dole out a few at a time. Before morning the cats got into the bucket and ate all the mice. Willie was heartbroken; his fun was spoiled.

Yes, we were sometimes hard up for amusement in the Stony Brook country. Radio had been invented, but not until the 1930s would Dad allow one of those newfangled things in the house. Even then he would not have one with a loudspeaker, so to listen to it we had to sit down and plug in earphones. We could listen only when doing such jobs as hand sewing, shelling peas, or peeling potatoes.

Mama had a piano, Dad a violin, and they both had a number of good books and subscribed to several magazines. Mama taught us poems and songs, Dad interested Bud and me in history, Grover and Dad taught us about nature and animals.

About 1924 a rural telephone line had been put in the area at the expense of the local residents. Until then the way to send a message was "put a kid on a horse." When telephones came, each rural neighborhood had a party line composed of several neighbors. Each small town had a switchboard run by "Central," who was usually the wife of the man who maintained the telephone lines. All calls except those between the individuals on a party line went through Central.

Centrals and maintenance men worked under a telephone company supervisor who came around to each small town occasionally. The supervisor in our area told with glee the story (whether apocryphal, I don't know) of the time he reprimanded Dave, the local maintenance man. A crabby old maid in the west part of town had put in a complaint that Dave, while working on the line in front of her house, had used bad language.

"Oh, no," Dave protested. "I wouldn't use bad language in front of a fine lady like Miss Alexander. I'll tell you just what happened. Johnny was on top of the pole soldering an insulator and dropped some hot solder down the back of my neck. I looked up at him and said, 'Really, Johnny, you ought to be more careful.' "

We had wall telephones with a crank at the side to ring them. All rings were heard by everyone on the party line. Everyone knew just who was being called because each ring was different. Ours, I recall, was a long ring followed by a short ring. The Scotts were called by three short rings and one Brewer family by two longs and two shorts. It did not matter who was called; all the neighbors listened in. This was called "rubbernecking" and was the main amusement and diversion of the rural housewife.

Central, a vital part of the community, always knew where everybody was and what was going on. In case of disaster or emergency, such as "Johnsons' little boy is missing" or "Hannan's barn is on fire," Central used the general ring, a series of long rings, to summon the people on all the party lines to drop what they were doing and go to help.

During World War I three families—the Scotts and the two Brewer brothers—bought land in the section between our home section of 640 acres and the section of land we called our Big Pasture. They each bought 160 acres on mortgages which, when prices fell after the war, they were never able to pay. In the two Brewer families were children about our ages with whom we had fun attending school together, playing, and having picnics.

Bud and I enjoyed working with horses and cattle and almost all outdoor work. Ethel cared nothing for animals or the outdoors but liked to play the piano and spent much of her school vacation time visiting away from home, most frequently at the home of Mama's sister Alice, who had an adult son but no daughter.

Much of the work Bud and I did was with horses. In spare time we rode horses for pleasure and to enjoy the countryside. We had a few saddle horses to work cattle and about fourteen draft horses to do farm work.

When I was a little girl, my father rode a big sorrel stallion named Saul, widely noted in North Dakota as a fine horse. When Saul died, Dad hung up his bridle and never used it again. Then his saddle horse was Dakota Belle. She was full of tricks. It took ingenuity to devise gate or door fastenings she couldn't open. When a high wind was blowing, and only then, she loved to grab Dad's hat brim in her teeth and toss his hat into the wind. You could fairly see her laughing as Dad ran to retrieve his hat. Of course she knew the trick of taking a deep breath and holding it as the saddle was cinched so that the cinch would be loose.

For a number of years my saddle horse was the ornery bronco named Pronto. She had a colt named Piute that I broke to ride when she was three years old. Piute was a good horse but had little personality. Bud once said, "Piute reminds me of a sick owl. She just doesn't give a hoot."

The summer of 1928 was very wet. Crops and hayfields were lush; mosquitoes were thick and a continual torture to us and the livestock. Bud and I were milking eight cows twice a day. I raised chickens but lost many of them to skunks, hail, and rain. We kept the pullets for laying hens and a few roosters for breeding purposes. Most of the roosters we ate. The rest I sold, saving the money for future college expenses.

Dad and Mama wanted Ethel and me to go to a private Presbyterian college of high scholastic rating in Jamestown, North Dakota, the county seat thirty miles from home. Tuition was much higher there than at state-run colleges, so the folks told me I must win a scholarship to pay my tuition for four years because otherwise they could not afford to send us both. I was keeping my high school grades the highest in order to win the scholarship and raising chickens in the summers to save money toward our college expenses. Dad had started Bud a herd of cattle of his own. Bud would be ready for college a year before Ethel and I were through. Back at that time we thought we could manage because Bud, at college age, would have his own little herd.

On Sunday, July 1, 1928, a devastating hailstorm struck our section of the state. Although the hay crop was not hurt much, most of the other crops, including my Uncle Grover's, were a total loss. Dad still had some oats, a little barley, and some seed wheat. Everything else was gone, including forty acres of seed sweet clover. We had sorely needed the income from that seed.

The rest of the summer was a nightmare of slogging through either rain or clouds of mosquitoes to salvage what we could from the land and to take care of poultry and livestock. Bud said North Dakota never did anything by halves. It was either too wet or too dry. Bud got no vacation except that on his birthday, July 4, Dad took him to the county fair. I got a weekend in late August.

August 29, 1928, Wednesday

Last Friday I rode Pronto to visit Mama's youngest sister, Nona. Cutting across country it is only about twelve miles. After the work was done Friday night, and the kids asleep, Nona and I sat up talking until 10:30. Uncle Amos was at the pool hall in town.

Saturday I herded the sheep. They belong to Aunt Nona; she didn't let Uncle Amos mortgage them when he mortgaged everything else. The bank sold them out last fall. She bid one horse back, and a neighbor bid one back for her. She managed to bid back one cow, but the good ones went.

Nona had been working in the hay field. Since some men were helping Saturday, she stayed home. I don't think a woman ought to do all the chores, keep house, raise poultry and a garden, care for three small children, and work in the fields, too. Nona always did work hard. She was the youngest of her family. When she was about sixteen her father mortgaged the farm to buy another half section. A few months later he was killed in an accident. Since the other children were grown up and gone, Nona took over running the farm, paid off the mortgage in a few years, and saved $3000.00 for her mother. A banker once remarked that Nona could teach most men a lot about farming. What man is ever willing to listen to a woman?

Nona, with her beauty and personality, had many chances to marry. She chose Uncle Amos. Though her relatives disapproved of her choice and disapprove of the way he treats Nona, they have, for her sake, always been nice to him. She is always cheerful and hopeful, but she is coping with a mess he made. In 1919 Uncle Amos mortgaged his property to buy another farming outfit. This was against Nona's wishes and just as the farming boom of the World War was busting. A second outfit meant hiring a man to run the machinery and buying feed for extra horses. Low prices have made it impossible to pay the mortgage. Last fall the bank foreclosed. Nona says she hopes they can operate on a small scale and get on their feet again.

Saturday night Nona, Uncle Amos, the kids, and I went to town, Pingree, where he went to the pool hall and she traded her eggs and cream for some groceries and gas for the car.

Sunday they were still haying. I herded the sheep. Mrs. Farr, a neighbor, came over and helped fix a fried chicken dinner for us and the two men who were helping with the hay.

In the afternoon Nona had to work in the hayfield. Mrs. Farr and I did the dishes and baked bread. About 3:00 P.M. rain stopped the haying. It rained all night. I was supposed to go home Sunday, but it rained so hard I stayed over.

Nona and I did the milking and other chores Monday morning and got breakfast. The answer to the maiden's prayer got up in time to eat—with a grouch wonderful to behold. He had been in the pool hall very late. I'm glad Dad and his brothers don't chew tobacco, drink, or hang around pool halls.

Until late afternoon Nona and I washed clothes. Then I found the place the sheep were getting out and fixed the fence. Uncle Amos was spending the day in the pool hall.

Pronto, rested and cutting up, came home at a good clip. She reminded me of the story Cousin Harry told about the Irishman and the bucking horse. When the horse got its hoof caught in the stirrup, the man said, "B' Gorry, if you're gonna get on, I'm gonna get off!"

There is nothing more recorded in my diary until late October.

October 26, 1928, Friday

Due to repair work, school didn't start until September 17. None of the high school teachers came back, so we have three new ones, and no Latin teacher. I'm taking citizenship, shorthand, typing II, English III, U.S. history, and physical education.

It would be nice if we would move to town soon. With studying, work at home, and driving back and forth, I'm busy from 5:30 A.M. until 10:30 P.M. I bought a Royal portable typewriter badly needed for school work, but it cost $60.00 of college savings.

On November 6, I noted that was the day either Herbert Hoover or Al Smith would be elected president. Dad thought the farmers would get no help from either. He said that because of government monkey business the railroads were allowed to set freight rates too high on everything the farmer had to ship in and out of Dakota, and the buyers of beef and wheat set arbitrary prices the farmer had to take.

It was not so bad if a farmer chose his profession. If he went into it for the reason Dad did, it was an unsatisfying life. Dad, his father, and his grandfather were not destined for farming. We assume Dad's grandfather was a farmer in the small community in western New York state where he lived. After the death of his wife, when his son, Dad's father, was three years old, Great-grandfather left his son with his wife's relatives (he had none) and headed west. He was a prospector in California in 1849 and 1850, then a guide for wagon trains until increasing civilization ended that as a profitable job, then a prospector again until accidentally killed near Last Chance Gulch, Montana Territory, in 1878. He made a fair amount of money. Being a very religious man, he did not squander it on what he considered the sins of his contemporaries—drink, gambling, and Indian wives. He sent his money back to New York to provide his son with the best the time and place afforded. The puritanical man was horrified when he found out his son was studying, among other subjects, art and the violin.

"Artists are poor as church mice," he declared, "and fiddlers are aides of the Devil!"

Teachers at the seminary mollified him by pointing out that art and music can be used to the glorification of God.

Dad's father was educated to be a minister. Before he was ordained, a doctor warned him that he was threatened with tuberculosis (called consumption of the lungs in those days, and invariably fatal) and advised an outdoor life. Great-grandfather bought him a farm in Minnesota. There he met and married Grandma, whose people had moved to Minnesota after the Civil War.

Grandpa didn't care for farming but was a good carpenter who could design as well as construct. After his crops were planted in

Minnesota, he habitually made trips to Dakota Territory doing construction work in towns along the expanding railway system. A number of buildings he erected still stand.

Dakota Territory struck him as a place of wonderful opportunity because of the cheap land available. Finally, in the early 1880s, he sold his farm in Minnesota for money to establish his family in the Territory. On the homestead he built a two-story frame house—quite a luxury in the days when most homesteaders had only tarpaper shacks or sod houses.

Grandpa had acquired three quarter-sections of land, 480 acres, composed of the homestead, a pre-emption, and a tree claim. Under the Homestead Act of 1862 a settler was given 160 acres in public domain for living on the land and cultivating a portion of it for five years. He paid fees of only $14.00 when he made the original entry on the land and $4.00 when he "proved up," that is, proved he had fulfilled the requirements, and received title to the land. Under the Pre-emption Act of 1841, repealed in 1891, a settler could buy 160 acres in public domain for $1.25 an acre after living on the land for six months and making certain improvements. Under the Timber Act, passed in 1873 and repealed in 1891, a settler could acquire 160 acres by planting 10 acres of it to trees. The entry fee was $14.00; there was no residence requirement. To prove up on his tree claim at the end of eight years, the settler had to have 675 living trees on each of the ten acres.

Grandpa's high hopes and hard work met with continual discouragement. The disaster of summer drouths in the 1880s was coupled with bitterly cold winters. Crops failed year after year, and prices were low. Oats sold for 13¢ a bushel, fat cows for $15 apiece, eggs for 7¢ a dozen. He hauled water for miles trying to save the trees on his tree claim, but so many died he failed to meet the requirements and lost it. Hard times forced him to sell his pre-emption rights. He was left with the 160-acre homestead. Nestled in the hills beside the river, it had a beautiful setting but failed to provide a living. He had intended to raise just livestock on that piece of land but could not afford to stock it.

Providing food, clothing, coal, and other necessities for his growing family was a problem. Grandma raised a garden and fruit. Wild game helped provide meat. As fast as they could get milk cows and poultry, variety was added to the menu. In the winter or whenever not needed for farm work, Grandpa did carpentry. Since the horses were needed at home, he would pack his tools on his back and walk long miles to work. From Pingree, seven miles away, he would carry home on his back sacks of flour and other things his family needed. The family finally totaled eleven children, though Grandpa never saw the youngest.

There was no doctor near enough to be of any help. Grandma had none for childbirth and had to tend all the children's illnesses and injuries herself. She must have been good at it; the children all lived to healthy adulthood. Some families were not so lucky. In the 1920s I met an elderly woman who had been one of the homesteaders. She told me that in the 1880s she lost all five of her children in an epidemic one winter. "The Lord was good to me," she added. "He sent me five more."

As there were no schools close enough for the children to attend, Grandma and Grandpa taught from their own books and gave religious instruction. Grandpa played his violin and drew pictures to entertain them. Each Christmas and Easter he planned programs and taught them their parts.

Early one December morning in 1889 the house burned. The family fled with whatever clothes and blankets they could snatch as they went, while Dad and Grandpa carried the two youngest children out in their beds. Everything else they possessed, including the winter's supply of food, burned up.

Neighbors shared shelter and supplies. The irreplaceable losses to the children were the books with their glimpses of the outside world, the violin, which provided the only music they had ever heard, and Grandpa's paintings and sketches that gave them a view of the world of art.

Grandpa mortgaged his homestead for the money to build a new house. The 1890s were going to be better. By that time they had acquired more horses and cattle and there was more rainfall, giving hope of good crops. Grandpa, in harvest time, could work as a separator man on a threshing crew for $5.00 a day, which was more than carpentry paid. Dad, a teenager with a team of horses, could work as a harvest teamster for $2.50 a day. A rural school within a few miles gave the children a chance to go to school.

The schoolhouse was a rectangular building with three long rows of seats and a teacher's desk in front. Pupils had to furnish their own books. These were usually books that had belonged to their parents, so few books in a class ever matched. Most of the pupils never went beyond the fourth grade. The teacher had to pass the eighth grade and take an examination, which was not very difficult, to get a teaching certificate. School was held only during the three summer months each year.

The 1890s may have started out well but were not really better. The panic of 1893 struck the whole country and drouth hit again in North Dakota, which had attained statehood in 1889. Dad and his oldest sister, Em, had reached college age and longed to go to college to fit themselves for a different life. They had not even had a chance to go to high school. Grandpa wished with all his heart to give his children the opportunities his own father had given him. However, he had not been able to pay off the mortgage and had no money to send his two oldest children away to school. He could not even see a chance to send the younger ones as they became old enough.

So things went through the decade of the 1890s. Near the end of that decade the family was left fatherless shortly before Ted, the youngest, was born.

Dad and Em were stuck. They worked very hard. Em worked away from home in the winters, sending her money home to help with living expenses and the acquisition of more land. In the summers she came home and helped her mother with the staggering amount of housework, garden work, poultry raising, and the preservation of food for winter. She also mothered the younger children when her frantically busy mother had no time. Her sewing ability in those days when she had to make her own patterns, her skill at "making over" and "making do," were important factors in keeping the family clothed. Meanwhile Dad ran the homestead.

As the years went on, Grandpa's hopes were fulfilled. The mortgage was paid and enough more land purchased to bring the crop and pasture land to 520 acres, a profitable unit. Dad and Em did not have a college education, but the other nine children did.

At the age of twenty-one, when Dad could legally file on his own homestead, he chose an L-shaped tract to include the "Big Spring." Control of the water would preclude other homesteaders from crowding in around him. As his three oldest sisters became old enough, he had them file on adjoining tracts he later bought from them, giving him the 640 acres where we lived. For extra pasture he leased 640 acres, a school section of state land with the James River running through it. We called it the Big Pasture. He bought 200 acres of land at Arrowwood Lake, later selling 120 acres of it to Grover, who incorporated it into his ranch, called "Pelican Roost."

Dad did not marry until he was thirty-six years old. There was probably neither time nor money any sooner. With all those younger brothers and sisters he had to help his mother raise and educate, the job of paying off the mortgage on the homestead and acquiring more land to make it a paying farm, and the task of looking after his own homestead and those of his sisters, Dad must have been as busy as a one-armed man saddling a bronco.

November 6, 1928

Dad never wanted to be a farmer, but now, in his 50's, is still caught up in the everlasting struggle. He and Mama raised her motherless niece. He has three children of his own to educate. Actually, he was quite prosperous for many years until recently. Now times are hard, prices low, and this year we are hailed out. I guess he will manage. He always has.

Come to think of it, Dad never plays his violin any more. Before Grandpa's violin burned up, he taught Dad a little about playing it. Years later Dad bought one, though he never could read a note of music. If he could whistle a tune, he could play it. Winter evenings he used to get out his violin and play a long time. But not these last few years. I guess a man gets old and tired.

In mid-November John and Theresa came back. Mama, Ethel, Bud, and I moved to rented rooms in the town of Kensal. For the job of moving I wanted to wear my boy's shirt, pants, and boots I wore on the farm. Dad would not let me, saying it was bad enough that I wore boy's clothes at home; to go to town I must put on a dress and look respectable. I grumbled in my diary, "When I grow up I'll wear pants all I want to!"

Kensal was a town started in 1892 when the Minneapolis, Milwaukee, and Sault Ste. Marie Railroad (known as the Soo) was built through there. Other towns in the area we sometimes visited were Pingree and Edmunds to the west of us, both founded about 1880 when the Northern Pacific (now the Burlington Northern) ran a branch north of Jamestown.

In 1928 Kensal had a population of about four hundred. Pingree and Edmunds were a bit smaller. In those days of poor roads and slow cars, when much of the traveling was done with horses, each town supported a number of business places.

There were three churches—Lutheran, Methodist, and Catholic—in Kensal. We had an eight-room school for grade and high school, employing seven teachers—four in the grade school and three in the high school. The business places included a tow mill (where a material called tow was made from flax straw), a bank, three grain elevators, a lumberyard, hardware store, hotel, restaurant, drugstore, blacksmith shop, butcher shop, harness shop, weekly paper, livery barn, pool room, and one doctor. In addition there was a cream station, two grocery stores, a farm implement dealer who also sold Chevrolet automobiles, a dentist, a movie theater and dance hall, and two general merchandise stores commonly known as "mercantile stores." These sold just about anything from groceries and dry goods to kerosene lamps and ax handles.

When I was young, the farmers took their surplus cream to town to sell at the cream station, which paid according to butterfat content and shipped the cream on to butter-making companies. Surplus eggs were traded for groceries. Some farm wives made butter to trade at the stores or sell to private customers in town. Farm people raised most of their food. Purchases were usually only tea, coffee, yeast, baking soda, spices and flavoring, baking powder, fresh fruit if it could be afforded, gasoline and kerosene in barrels, and flour and sugar in hundred-pound sacks. Those sacks were useful. From them we made dishtowels, aprons, underwear, pillowcases, and even sheets. There was no such thing as a self-service store. We went in with a list we read to the clerk, who brought the goods to the counter to box or bag for us.

Jamestown, our county seat thirty miles away, had a population of about five thousand and much more variety in the stores. Before school started each fall we went to Jamestown to buy shoes, stockings, and dress goods at Penney's. I loved that store. Besides the fascinating stock of goods to see, it was fun to watch the little baskets. Metal baskets or canisters hung on a wire over each counter. The clerk would put our money and sales slip in the basket and pull a lever to send it up the wire to an office on the balcony. A girl up there would put our change and receipt in the basket, which came sliding back down the wire.

November 18, 1928

It is lucky I bought the typewriter. The rest of my money is gone. The bank failed last Friday, so the whole community is pretty blue. Since the July I hailstorm farmers have drawn out more than $50,000 and had nothing to put in. Now the money, some of it borrowed, they counted on for living expenses this winter and for seed grain in the spring is gone.

Our student association lost the $124.00 we had made to pay for basketball suits. The teachers lost any money they had. Miss Lundeen is left with 15¢ and in debt for clothes she charged in Minneapolis.

I'm sorry for the janitor and his wife. Since Bart lost his farm to a mortgagee, he bought a little shack in town and works as school janitor and general handyman around town. He never could afford to fix up the shack, so for two years his wife has worked seven days a week, eighteen hours a day, as a cook during threshing season. She saved her money to fix up the shack so that they would have a nicer home for their daughters.

I asked Dad what we will do now that the bank has failed. "Never mind, Doodler (his nickname for me) we'll pull out of this, but you better buy your shoes before I run out of money."

I won't use Dad's money for shoes and other things I need. The surplus chickens aren't sold yet. The Superintendent will pay me to do school typing and his personal typing after school and weekends. Typewriters are as scarce in this town as people who can type.

As for the bank failure, we hadn't, as the old slang phrase goes, "seen nothin' yet." But we somehow managed to make it that winter. Though prices were too low, Dad sold some of his steers instead of holding them in hope of a better price. Some money came in from chickens, hogs, and milk cows. We had all the meat, milk, eggs, potatoes, and butter we needed. When the hailstorm ruined the garden we had already canned some vegetables and still had such root crops as carrots, turnips, and rutabagas. Dad had bought fruit for us to can and, as usual in October, had purchased the winter's supply of coal, kerosene, gasoline, flour, and sugar. Principal cash expenses that winter were salaries for John and Theresa and the rent in town. By today's standards, those costs were very low.

Dad also got a small, very small, salary for acting as county commissioner. In 1923, when the county commissioner for our district died, Dad was appointed to finish the term. After that he ran for election every two years and was always elected, even though he never spent a penny campaigning. He enjoyed the job. It got him off the place occasionally. He was reimbursed for mileage, lunches, and telephone calls and was paid a small amount for attending meetings. Most months the commissioners took care of all county business in one or two days, though it took longer in January and July.

Of campaigning Dad would say, "Why spend the time and money? The people of this district know what I stand for. If they don't think I am right, they can vote me out." They never did. He was still commissioner when he died. Thirty years after his death, a Jamestown man, lamenting some local issues, said to me, "Ann, if your father was alive, these things wouldn't happen. He took care of public money like his own and influenced others to do the same." He recited, at length, accounts of things Dad had done to save taxpayers' money and still promote the public good.

I can remember one day in the 1930s when I, working out of earshot at the opposite end of the barn, noticed that Dad had a caller. It must have been about a county contract. As the man left, he raised his voice in anger: "You're a damn fool! You could have made a fast five hundred bucks here and no one would have known. And I know you need money."

I pricked up my ears for Dad's reply. In his soft, drawly voice, he said, "There is something I need more than money. I'll always be able to look an s.o.b. like you right square in the eye and tell you to go to hell."

December 29, 1928
As always on the day before Christmas I rode Pronto to Grandma's with presents for her and the boys and got theirs for us. Grover was getting hay in the meadow, so I rode over there and we talked and laughed for an hour. Grover is so much fun. Like Bud, he always has funny jokes and witty remarks.

Today was warm for this time of year, so I rode many miles in my beloved hills. Tonight I rode again. Under a full moon the south hills gleam white. Far away a coyote is howling in a silver world.

CHAPTER 2

Close to the Wind

Winter of 1928–29 was long, cold, and dreary. Except at
Christmas there was no opportunity to get home to my horses
and little to do for entertainment in town. If there was a quarter
to spare, one could go to the movie on Saturday night. Everyone
went to church Sunday mornings, and all the parents were careful
to see that the high school kids didn't sit in the same pew.
Epworth League for young people met at the church on Sunday
evenings. A popular pastime was a card game called whist, which
bored me. Mama did the small amount of cooking and housework
in our little apartment while we were in school. She and her
friends spent their spare time playing cards and doing crafts and
needlework. The church Ladies' Aid met twice a month and
Homemakers' Club once a month. She usually attended those
meetings.

I spent much of my time that winter typing for the superintendent, though he did not pay much. He probably could afford
very little, because he was supporting a family on $125 a month.
His wife often complained of how hard it was to get along on that.
Mama privately muttered she ought to be able to manage because
she knew exactly how much money was coming in—something a
farm wife never knew. The garage owner, who paid more, hired
me for what little typing work he had.

With school work and typing I should have been busy enough to keep out of mischief, but my diary indicates otherwise.

February 6, 1929
Fifth period today the shorthand teacher gave me a good mark and then said he had never seen me study. Indignant, as I get the highest marks in school, I told him the first period every day is my study period, and if he would look he would see me study.

"I do look. I see you whispering, or reading the newspaper over Dorothy's shoulder, or you and Buster are playing catch with ink bottles!"

Spring finally came.

May 4, 1929, Saturday
This afternoon I rode to Grandma's for a visit. It is such fun to visit Grandma and hear her stories of the early days here. She has had a very hard, but fascinating, life. Her house I just love: her bedroom furniture, including a bureau with a marble top and little button drawers above that; her living room with the intricately carved organ, a whole wall of bookshelves, paintings by Aunt Evalyn, handwoven draperies and pillow covers; her cozy kitchen; the dining room with its big oak table and Chinese vases and dishes. Aunt Elsie, since she went to China as a medical missionary in 1913, has been home twice, bringing Grandma many gifts from China. She has beautiful dishes and some very old vases, ornaments, and tapestries.

There is always the scent of baking and of lemon oil furniture polish at Grandma's house, and it is interesting to watch her blending scraps of wool or silk for her Log Cabin quilts, which are truly works of art.

May 29, 1929, Wednesday
After school today I had to mimeograph 300 letters and get them ready to mail. The principal came into the office and gabbed so much I asked him to lick the stamps and envelopes. That shut him up and got the work done faster.

Near the end of the school year there is a lot of typing to be done and end-of-the-month work for the garage owner. The money will come in handy to buy baby chickens. With school not letting out until June 7, I can't get enough chicks hatched out by setting hens, so I will buy 100 and hope to buy some turkey eggs to hatch under chicken hens.

When school let out, we moved back to the farm and John and Theresa left for their summer jobs. The long drouth had started. It was very dry and windy. Bud and I spent our time cultivating the corn, potato field, and garden while a large portion of the ranch dirt blew on us. Our evenings were spent doing chores, a repeat of the chores we did in the mornings before harnessing and hitching the horses to go to the fields. Laying hens, baby chicks and their mothers, and the hens setting on turkey eggs had to be fed and watered. We fed, watered, and curried the horses, went a mile to drive in the eight milk cows, grained and milked them, separated the milk, and fed and watered the calves and hogs. In the evenings, after gathering eggs from all over the place, we had to wash them and pack those to be sold. Later in the summer we would pack surplus eggs in waterglass-filled crocks in the basement for use when the hens quit laying in cold winter weather (waterglass was sodium silicate dissolved in water to make a syrupy liquid for preserving eggs).

Perhaps I should explain about separating the milk. In those days the cows were milked by hand and the milk was carried to the house and poured into a big steel bowl at the top of a machine called the separator. By hand we turned a crank at the side of the machine. That caused the milk to be driven through a series of numbered disks and through two spouts, one of which poured skim milk into the pails below and the other the cream. Whole milk had been saved out for household use. Skim milk was fed to calves, hogs, and chickens. We kept plenty of cream for our own use and for churning into butter. The rest was stored in five-gallon cans. When someone went to town, this sour cream was taken to be sold at the creamery, whence it was shipped to the Twin Cities in Minnesota to be made into butter. I never minded running the separator, but hated washing it. Twice a day the thing had to be taken apart and all the parts carefully washed and scalded and put back together, including the forty numbered disks, which had to be stacked together in proper order.

In 1928 we had plenty of rain but the crops were hailed out. In 1929 it just didn't rain. By late July the crops were scarcely worth harvesting. Dad had always had so much hay he let others put it up on shares and still always had a two-year supply. That year he and Bud and I put it up alone to ensure a two-year supply. We put it up in heat that ranged from 100° to 110° every day. Evenings we carried water in pails to the garden and flowers. We also kept moving the beef cattle to find enough pasture. Dad and I were worried. He had sold few steers the year before in hope of better prices in 1929. The drouth would force the sale of many cattle and depress prices still further. For years Dad and his brothers had been building up a good herd of Hereford breeding stock. Above all, we must save the bulls and brood cows.

Haying was tedious with the horse-drawn equipment farmers had then. Hay was cut in a six-foot swath and raked with a machine equipped with circular teeth and a pedal the driver stepped on to dump a pile of hay when the teeth were full. When it was cured enough, buck rakes picked up the hay to carry to the stack. These were usually homemade contraptions of about a dozen long wooden, metal-tipped, horse-drawn teeth to mesh with and drop the hay on the teeth of the stacker. The stacker was also a homemade contraption known as the "overshot stacker." After a buck rake load of hay was deposited on the stacker teeth, a long, stout rope pulled by a team of horses raised the teeth to dump the hay on the haystack. Depending on how many buck rakes were operating and over how large a territory, there would be one or two men on the stack to distribute the hay properly before another load came up.

Tuesday, June 25, 1929
As Bud and I cultivated corn this morning, Mama came out of the house waving a dishtowel as a signal for me to come home. The mailman had phoned that my crate of 100 baby chicks had come. He wanted me to meet him at the mailbox to get them. That is a mile

and a half from home, and Dad was away with the car.

The only way to get to the mailbox in time was lope up there on Pronto. I tied my cultivator team to the fence, threw a saddle on the mare, and made it in time. Then there was a little problem. Pronto keenly resents being used as a packhorse, and the "cheep-cheep-cheep" sounds from that crate did nothing for her nerves. I held her tightly enough to keep her from bucking or running away while the mailman helped me balance the crate on the saddle horn. Pronto did a war dance from one side of the road to the other all the way home. At home I could not dismount with the box, so I called Mama to come take it. She refused to go near the prancing horse. I rode to the field and had Bud remove the crate, then carried it to the barn, leading Pronto. The poultry companies add two or three chicks to each hundred to take care of death losses during shipment. Pronto and I got home with 103 chicks alive and healthy!

Dad says the last cream check came to over $6.00. That makes me feel better about working so hard with those cows.

Just for fun I have been sleeping outdoors, though there is not a lot of sleep to it. I take a purring cat to bed with me and lie there watching the moon and stars and listening to the night sounds. A south breeze brings the scent of hay from the meadow. From over the hills the coyotes sing to the stars. Sometimes I see the dawn break, and it is beautiful.

July 16, 1929, Tuesday

The temperature has been from 100 to 110 degrees every day. Today is Dad's birthday. He spent it putting up hay in 103-degree heat. This evening he sent me to the Big Pasture. The grass is still good in the flat, but the hills have none. I rode miles and lonely miles. Things don't look good.

Saturday night Dad took Bud and me to town with him and bought us ice cream for working so hard in the hayfield in this heat.

An entry in my diary a couple of weeks later gives a fairly complete description of the ranch.

August 1, 1929, Thursday

Coming back from the mailbox this morning, I stopped Pronto on the big hill a mile from home to look over the Stony Brook country. The road in front of me leads straight west through the hills and to the level land where Pingree and Edmunds are. The land beyond them is level clear to the distance-purpled Coteau du Missouri. To the southwest Stony Brook wends through and past our place in a meadow stretching for miles. Our buildings are on a knoll half a mile south of this road.

Grandma's place is more than two miles from ours on the west side of the river. Back of the northwest hills is the Big Flat containing the river, Arrowwood Lake, Mud Lake, Jim Lake, and Medicine Lake. This is my stamping ground. How I love it!

The only land of Dad's visible from this hill is the section, 640 acres, where the buildings are.

Half a mile in front of me our half-mile-long driveway leads from this road around a pasture where we keep milk cows and any draft and saddle horses needed at home. South of the pasture the driveway turns right and goes up a knoll to the buildings.

One spring, 1919 I think, water from melting snow flooded all the lowland. Our buildings were on an island for days. A man and team of horses trying to follow this road missed a curve and drowned. For weeks efforts were made to recover the man's body according to methods known at the time. A cannon was fired over the water to raise the body. It didn't. A soiled shirt of his was floated on the water with the supposition it would halt above his body. It didn't. After six weeks my Uncle Grover found it while out repairing a fence the flood had torn down.

Coming up the knoll to our buildings, one comes first to the corral, windmill, stock tank, loafing shed for beef cattle, and the barn. Dad has planted several rows of trees a quarter of a mile long northwest of the existing buildings. He intends to move his barn and feeding sheds out there when good times come again. Then the house will be the first building at the end of the driveway. As it is, we pass the other buildings first. The barn is a large one with stalls at one end for the horses and at the other end for the cows. There is an indoor watering trough and a pen in which to winter young calves. Above the barn is a hayloft. An attached large hayshed is on the north side. Hay is hauled in from the stacks during the winter, but Dad likes to keep plenty of feed at the barn in case blizzards prevent hauling hay.

The next building is the house. Dad and Mama started out with a five-room one-story house heated by coal stoves. As the family increased back when times were prosperous, Dad remodeled the house and replaced the cellar with a full basement containing a fruit room, furnace, big coal bin, and storage space. The bedroom that had adjoined the kitchen now houses laundry equipment, the cream separator, and outdoor clothing and boots. The downstairs now consists of that room, kitchen, large dining room, living room, and Mama and Dad's bedroom. The dining room is used as a living room much of the time because, while the other rooms are lighted by kerosene lamps, it has a gasoline Aladdin lamp giving much better light. We put the lamp in the middle of the dining room table during winter evenings to read, do school work, hand sewing, or play games by its light.

At the south side of the dining room is a stairway leading to three bedrooms and a bathroom. Ethel and I have the largest room, Bud and the hired help the other two. The hailstorm and bank failure kept Dad from getting running water and fixtures in the bath, so that room merely contains a chemical toilet for use in winter. In summer we use the outhouse. We bathe in a galvanized tub or take sponge baths. Mama believes in baths every night, but after long days of work and carrying water for other things, baths are apt to be sponge baths, which we refer to as "a lick and a promise."

Ivy climbs the walls outside the house. North of it is a lilac hedge, and a few trees and flowers are on all sides. What we call the kitchen garden is near the house. There we have currant bushes, rhubarb, horseradish, lettuce, radishes, and spring and winter onions. To the south of the knoll is a one-acre potato field and the main garden where the soil, in normal years, subirrigates. There we grow tomatoes, cucumbers, dill, beans, peas, swiss chard, beets, corn, cabbage, carrots, pumpkins, squash, parsnips, peppers, rutabaga, and strawberries. We have no fruit trees but get our apples and crabapples from Grandma's orchard.

Farther west and northwest are the garage and granaries; beyond them the calf pasture and shelterbelt of trees. The west and north part of the 640 acres is in field corn, alfalfa, and grain. The south part is all prairie hay meadow except for a 40-acre pasture north of the Big Spring. Dad's land at the lake is in grain. The Big Pasture, two *miles away, is only pasture land in hills, coulees, and a meadow with the James River running through it.*

After we finished haying, or interrupting the haying if the grain was ready, we harvested grain. Harvesting was done with a binder, a horse-drawn machine with a long cutting bar that cut the straw a few inches from the ground. Grain was carried across a canvas sheet and up a canvas elevator into a hopper, where it was compacted and tied in bundles with twine. When several bundles accumulated in the carrier into which the machine had dropped them, the man driving the four horses stepped on a foot lever which caused the carrier to drop the bundles to the ground.

To keep the grain from spoiling before it was threshed, we had to shock it. That meant walking around picking up the bundles, leaning two, grain heads up, propped against each other, eight or ten others propped around them tent style, and one laid over the top.

That summer of 1929 a relative gave me a mongrel puppy who had some shepherd blood and turned out to be a good cattle dog. I named him Kiyo. He was a medium-sized, long-haired mutt, mostly white with some black spots. Black patches around his eyes gave him a comical look. In spite of eight of the unfriendliest cats he ever saw, Kiyo liked our place and soon thought he was running it. If a hen wandered too far from the coop to suit him, he chased her back. When the men drove the calves out by day, he'd drive them back to the barn. When they convinced him they didn't want the calves back in, he'd drive them far off until convinced that was not what the men had in mind either.

Once Dad sold five big black hogs and bought five smaller white ones to fatten and sell. Kiyo, who always helped everyone whether they needed it or not, was so busy helping load the black hogs that he did not see the white ones unloaded. When he discovered them later, it was funny to see his bewilderment. He would run to the fence and cock his head to one side, looking at them, then run to Dad and whine. He could not understand why those creatures had changed size and color so suddenly.

He wanted to go everywhere the horses went and loved to tease Pronto by chasing around her and yapping. Every time her ears canted a certain way, he would dodge to avoid a kick. I told Dad that Kiyo must see some connection between the cant of Pronto's ears and her heels.

"Sure," he said. "There is a damned ornery bronco between them."

In August, 1929, while searching the Big Pasture for chokecherries to make jam and syrup, I found flags with the letters "USEO" and the words "Do not disturb." Some surveyors there told me the flags were to mark elevations for the Missouri River Diversion Project. The government was going to put in a big dam and divert the Missouri River for irrigation.

August 19, 1929, Wednesday
A frost the other night hit the tomatoes, corn, beans, and cucumbers. The brook is dry except immediately below the Big Spring. Dad says it never happened before in his lifetime.

When I left the barn tonight after the chores were done, the sunset was flashing opal over the rim of the hills and a full moon drifting up in the east. It was so beautiful I couldn't stay still, so I saddled up and rode out to look over the Stony Brook country and listen to the coyotes.

September 1, 1929, Sunday
At 4:00 this morning Dad came back from Grandma's with some grain wagons. The noise woke me up. "Ho! Hum!" I thought. "He has already driven his teams five miles before 4:00 A.M. No fun here Saturday night except for Kiyo, who argued with a coyote all night, and no sleep Sunday mornings. I bet Dad thinks it is high time I had the cows in, it being so late in the morning."

September 3, 1929, Tuesday
Frederickson's outfit came to thresh yesterday, but it rained just enough to stop them, so the crew went to town. They were so noisy when they returned that I wondered, as their shouts woke me, if they had imbibed too much hooch. This morning we learned that they

*came back to find fourteen turkeys in the bunk car. They herded them
into an empty bunk, but, when the turkeys wouldn't stay there,
chased them out.*

The bunk car was a long wooden shed on wheels, pulled by
horses from farm to farm to provide shelter for the threshing
crew, who slept in bunks built along the sides of the car. A similar
car was the cook car, which contained a cookstove and kitchen
equipment, a long table and benches where the crew ate, and a
bed for the cook.

By 1929, I think, the engines (tractors) used for threshing were
all gasoline-powered. Earlier they had been steam engines whose
fuel was wood to start the fire and straw to keep it going. One
man had to fire a steam engine continually. Another man, with a
horse-drawn water wagon, spent his time hauling water from the
nearest pond or stream. If the engineer was running low on steam,
one could hear him from miles away blasting the whistle to hurry
up the water wagon.

The separator, a machine about thirty feet long, was powered
by a big belt running from the tractor. A separator man looked
after it—a diabolical machine with something always going wrong.
It consisted of a feeder, or conveyor which carried the bundles of
grain into a cylinder where cutting and beating teeth separated the
kernels from the straw, and next, a winnowing section where a fan
blew the chaff and straw away from the grain. The grain fell into
an elevator which lifted it and poured it into the waiting grain
wagon. The straw moved to a blower that blew it out into a stack.
Straw was used for bedding the animals. Surplus stacks were
burned in the spring. A time came when straw had to be used as
feed, but it was not nourishing.

The man who owned the threshing machine hired a crew and
moved from farm to farm. In addition to the help mentioned
above, he would hire ten or twelve bundle haulers with teams and
wagons.

The grain would have been bound in bundles and set up in
shocks. Bundle men drove their wagons around the field picking
up the shocks with pitchforks. When his wagon was loaded, the
driver would head for the separator. A man called the "spike

pitcher" stayed in the field all the time helping load the wagons.

Wagons, one on each side of the separator, were unloaded continuously. The bundles had to be forked into the machine carefully—not too fast or too slow—and lying lengthwise, not crosswise—else they would gum up the machine. If a bundle man happened to lose his pitchfork into the separator, it really played hob.

The grain, being dry, could be threshed earlier in the morning than the present-day combine can cut standing grain. The men worked from dawn until dark. In the summer dawn comes very early in North Dakota, and dark very late. By full daylight the men had to have the horses fed, watered, curried, and harnessed, the wagon wheels greased, and their breakfast eaten.

The man owning the farm had to furnish the grain haulers. Neighbors pooled wagons and manpower to help each other. It took six horses to pull the larger grain wagons. When one was filled at the separator, the driver either took the grain to a granary on the farm for later use or sale or else hauled it to the grain elevator in town for immediate sale.

When we saw a grain wagon headed for town, we knew a meal must be ready for the driver in seven hours. It would take him that long to get there and back. (Now, in a truck, the farmer's wife or a child old enough to drive can make it in twenty minutes.)

If the wagon unloaded at a granary on the farm, the grain usually had to be shoveled up into the bins by hand. We had an elevator powered by a gasoline engine. As grain ran out of the wagon into the hopper, a moving chain of disks moved it up a metal trough into the bins. Little shoveling was required because a trap door at the back of the wagon let most of the grain into the hopper by gravity flow.

The thresher furnished a bunk car where his crew slept and a cook car where they ate. The farmer had to supply feed for the horses as long as they were on his place, and all the potatoes the cook needed. All other food for the crew was furnished by the thresher.

The farmer's wife provided dinner (the noon meal) and sometimes supper for the grain haulers. The meals were lavish. A farm wife would have disgraced herself and her husband if she had not prepared a good meal—platters of fried chicken as well as either a beef or pork roast, heaping bowls of mashed potatoes, several kinds of vegetables from her garden, homemade bread or rolls, butter, jelly and jam, pickles, pies, and cake.

Bruce Quade, west of Pingree, had a combine in 1929, a new machine that saved time and manpower by cutting and threshing the grain in one operation. Straw was cut higher than it could be with a binder and scattered out on the ground. Grain went into a hopper from which it was periodically unloaded into a grain wagon. The whole harvesting and threshing operation could be done by two men, exclusive of grain haulers, one on the tractor and one on the combine. Much time and hard work was saved.

Our crops in 1929 were worse than the year before when destroyed by hail. One hundred acres of flax made only three bushels to the acre, with straw so short Bud had to cut it with a mower instead of the binder.

Flax is a beautiful crop. The stems are a shade of green differing from anything else we grew. When it blooms, the whole field is a sea of blue. As it ripens the stalks turn brown, topped by little brown bolls containing the tiny, and much darker brown, seeds. It took a lot of seeds to make a bushel, but each bushel was valuable. It could be sold either for seed or for making linseed oil, with the residue made into cakes for livestock feed.

We used to raid the flaxseed bin in the granary for medicine. A flaxseed slipped under the eyelid forms a mucus that soothes the eye and gathers up dust or any foreign object in the eye. Flaxseed tea, sweetened with honey, was used for colds or rheumatism, and a flaxseed poultice was the remedy for congestion of the chest or a sty on the eyelid.

That fall of 1929 one of Dad's long-held ambitions began to be fulfilled. The "north road," an old prairie road half a mile north of us, which ran ten miles east from Edmunds to meet Highway 9, where we turned north to Kensal, was being rebuilt and graveled. About half the work was done that fall. The old road was certainly not suited for automobile travel.

The contractor had a camp he moved as the work progressed. He had his own power plant for electric lights, three big tent barns, a herd of horses and mules, a number of bunk cars, a cook car, office car, blacksmith shop, dump wagons, fresnos, and some Caterpillar tractors.

The fresno is a machine of the past, and I do not even find the word in my dictionary. It was a large metal scoop drawn by four horses and used to dig up dirt to grade the road. One man drove the horses and another handled the long lever by which the machine was raised and lowered to scoop up and then dump out the loads of dirt.

When school started that fall, until November when John and Theresa came back and we moved to town, life was hectic. The superintendent hired me to do his typing again, but until we moved to town there was no time to do it except the noon hour and my so-called study period. At home Bud and I were rushed to death. Mama was sick in bed and Dad had all he could do tending horses and field work.

September 12, 1929, Thursday
Mama worries that Bud and I have too much to do, especially when she is sick. It is Mama who has too much to do, at least when Bud and I are in school. All the housework and cooking is an awful lot of work. When we aren't here, she tends the poultry and garden, too. Dad always used to hire a woman to help her. Now he can't afford it or even hire the help badly needed for farm work. This year he and Bud and I did it all.

Near the end of September I reported that Mama was getting better and could prepare breakfast and do the dishes. In the evenings Bud and I could manage the chores and cooking at a slower pace. In the mornings, however, before we left for school at eight o'clock, we had to go half a mile for the milk cows, drive them home, grain and milk them, separate the milk, wash and dry the separator, feed and water nine calves, the hogs, a dog, the cats, more than two hundred chickens and forty turkeys, prepare and eat breakfast, and get cleaned up to drive the seven miles over bad roads to school. If we had a few minutes left, we swept floors, made beds, did the dishes, and emptied the cream into a can for shipping.

September 28, 1929, Saturday

My chum Edith didn't get to school until nearly noon yesterday. Before school she had to take her brother to Guenthers', where he is helping put up hay. That is 12 miles over roads that are no speedways. On the way home she had to stop and pump up a tire three times. When she got home and fixed the tire, she failed to allow enough time for the patching cement to dry properly. While she was eating a bite and preparing for school, the tire went down again, and again she had to patch it.

I sometimes think I have a struggle to get to school in the fall before we move to town. Edith has it all the time. She drives four miles to school all winter long. If she can't drive, she walks. Her father is dead. Her mother lost all her money in the bank failure. Her brother, with what help Edith can give him, runs the farm and works out for cash.

Mr. Hokinson was fixing the telephone line today and had dinner with us. He and Dad discussed the Farmers Union starting up here. They agree the idea is all right, but some of the people controlling it are not and are apt to bring disaster to it locally. Our neighbor Len has been advocating it. One day last winter when Dad was hauling wheat to town by team and wagon, he saw ahead of him Len haranguing old Hans, who was out by his mailbox. By the time Dad got there, Len was gone and Hans still standing by the mailbox deep in thought.

"What's the matter, Hans?"

"I like for folks to mind dere own damn business."

Dad laughed. "I didn't mean to be butting into your business."

"Oh, God Yesus, I not mean you! I mean dese young fellers vat move in here and tell old-timers vat to do. I not like it. Ve all be better off if dey don't start farming here in de first place. Dis vas cattle country."

I rode to the road contractor's outfit today. He is now as far as the hills north of the Big Pasture. There were three Caterpillars at work, horses and mules, and pick and shovel men. He uses mules more than horses because they can stand heat better and are not ruined by the carelessness of the men in feeding them.

It will be nice when the road is finished. The present one is pretty bad, though I don't have any trouble getting the Model T over it until the snow is really deep. Mud never seems to faze the Ford. Dad used to have a big touring car. Because the Model T is so much simpler to handle and repair, he traded for it when I started driving us to town to school. He intended to buy a new touring car for himself but hasn't been able to afford it. I just hope the Model T keeps running until good times come again. If it doesn't, we are out of luck. Even as it is, I have to drive the kids to school in the horse and buggy several days each fall when Dad is at Commissioners' meetings. It costs 25¢ a day to have the horse and buggy taken care of at the livery stable.

Last night I stayed awake a long time enjoying the coyotes singing up in the hills. Their songs are beautiful and unique. They seem to throw their voices—they can sound far away or very near, and just one coyote can sound like several part of the time, and like a single singer the rest of the time.

November 2, 1929, Saturday

Last weekend a bad blizzard struck and it snowed so much all week we couldn't get to school at all. Dad and Bud and I had a real struggle getting the cattle in from the hills in that blinding snow.

Dad said it reminded him of the winter of 1896–97 when rain on the 28th of October turned into a blizzard. Dad killed the best horse he ever rode getting his cattle home. Coal had not yet been shipped into the state. There was some at Pingree, but it took men days to get it. John Roach was gone a week. Meanwhile his wife burned furniture and grain to keep from freezing and walked the floor in anxiety lest John be lying frozen along the road somewhere. Some men had to haul coal home on handsleds. The snow kept coming; winter lasted until May. Fences and houses were buried under deep drifts and the coulees were level with the hills.

The contractor, of course, has had to quit road work until spring. Machines are the coming thing, so he is disposing of his mules and horses. Dad bought a team called Jim and Jumbo—the biggest horses I ever saw. Their harnesses came with them because they are too big for any but especially made harnesses and collars.

Today the barn boss brought them down here to me, telling me they are as gentle as kittens and I will love them. It is obvious the old man hates to see them go. I know how he feels.

I did love those perfect pets. When they were hitched to something, it moved. One day that winter John, the hired man, had to take the team to pull out a truck loaded with hay and hopelessly stuck on the road north of us. One of the men with the truck was inclined to make fun of the big horses, saying, "If I had a team like that, I'd go after my hay one day and home the next."

"If you had a team like this," John retorted, "you would be sure of getting home."

In the spring, when the contractor came back to finish the road, Jim and Jumbo would prick up their ears and champ at their bits when they heard the machines. The barn boss never came to see them. Perhaps he, too, had been phased out.

November 9, 1929, Saturday

It is still cold and snowy. John and Theresa are back, so we moved to town last weekend.

There seems to be quite a furor in the country over a big stock market crash that wiped a lot of people out. We are ahead of them. The hailstorm in July of 1928 and bank failure that fall wiped out a lot of people locally. As far as that goes, most of North Dakota was hard hit last year.

Due to low prices Dad has decided to keep his cattle over winter. A lot of people have to sell for lack of feed. Dad and Bud and I put up plenty of hay. Maybe next year we won't have to work so hard. There may be plenty of rain and hay. Cattle prices may go up.

John brought us home last night in the bobsled. When the snow is too deep for a car, Dad and Bud and I can always get around on horseback. Mama and Ethel never learned to ride. To transport them Dad fixes up a bobsled, though that makes for a slow, cold journey they will seldom consent to take. He fastens one of the grain boxes from a wagon onto big sleigh runners drawn by a team of powerful, but slow, draft horses. In the wagon box he piles straw and blankets and steer hides to keep us warm. Since Mama is especially susceptible to cold, he gives her his buffalo hide overcoat and fixes the foot-warmer, a metal box covered with carpeting and with a drawer to hold hot coals, so she can keep her feet toasty warm.

Dad says the sheriff has an order from a bank to kick Grover Stern off his farm. He lost the place to a bank in the Twin Cities, but has a herd of sheep mortgaged to another bank down there. One bank told him to move; the other told him to stay there and look after the sheep. Now the bank foreclosing on the farm has put the sheriff on the job. I wonder what the other bank will do about the sheep.

Thank goodness, Dad hates mortgages and won't mortgage this place come hell or high water. These mortgaged farms! Old Man Ziets was living on one. He got a crop of one bushel to the acre. While he was harvesting last fall, the bankers owning the mortgage drove out in the field and bawled him out for not having a better crop.

Ziets stepped off the binder. "Chentlemen, here you are. Chust help yourselfs." He walked off the field and off the farm.

A man who had the mortgage on them came and took the horses. Another mortgagee took the machinery. The bankers had a hard time getting the grain harvested.

Ziets hopped a freight train to Montana, where he is mining or lumbering or something.

Winter seems to have come to stay. After the driest summer in Dakota history, winter has to start in October! It means a long feeding season.

This outfit is driving me nuts this evening. None of us can ever talk to each other. Bud has gone to bed and isn't trying to talk to anybody. Mama is trying to talk to Dad about some gossip she heard at Homemakers' Club. He isn't listening because he is trying to talk to her about the calf crop. I went upstairs to talk to Ethel about some school work, but she isn't listening because she is raving about how Lyle Brewer is now her boy friend. None of us listen to each other. If I wanted to say anything, I could tell her she is Lyle's second choice. He's been trying to get me to be his girl friend.

December 26, 1929, Thursday
It is still very cold with lots of snow. School let out for Christmas vacation last Friday for only a week. That is o.k. because it is too cold to go riding. I just listen to the wind howling and watch, through a little space I've cleared on the frosted window, the snow blowing across the prairie and Dad and Jim and Jumbo—all three coated with frost—hauling in hay for the cattle.

Lyle took Ethel to Jamestown for the first talking movie there, The

Desert Song. *She said it was wonderful. Conversation in movies has always been shown by brief printed captions below the pictures. Now one can actually hear the actors speak and sing songs. Until now the movie theaters have hired pianists to play music fitting the pictures, such as a love song where appropriate or a blood and thunder theme if the scene is a battle.*

CHAPTER 3

The Squall

Bad weather and roads prevented our getting home again until late spring. Meanwhile Mama had not been feeling well and consulted a doctor in Valley City. He advised an appendectomy, which she had in Valley City in late April, 1930.

She had planned to make graduation dresses for Ethel and me, sleeveless for the banquet and with capes or jackets so we could wear same dresses for graduation. Of course, she was unable to do it, but I got a big typing job for the American Legion and made enough money to buy us each a pair of pretty shoes and each a dress of the type Mama had planned. An old snapshot shows that years later I was still wearing mine for best. In May I wrote:

*Dad and I have been discussing what we will do this summer.
Chickens are so unprofitable we have decided to concentrate on
turkeys. They bring about $5.00 apiece on the Thanksgiving and
Christmas markets. The trouble is we don't have suitable sheds and
pens for them and can't afford any. Dad plans to cobble up
something. He can't afford any help. We'll manage.*

*I asked him about getting Sunday evenings off. He said we will talk
about it later. You bet we will!*

Ethel has a new boy friend, Winthrop, but the folks just do not approve of him. They wish Ethel showed more interest in education. Mama's heart is set on good educations for her children. Dad wants that, too, and wants to hang onto the ranch to turn over to Bud in the future.

Bud and I would like just good times and nice clothes, perhaps as much as Ethel does, but above all we intend to look after this ranch and to go to college. He wants to go to the Agricultural College and take animal husbandry, farm economics, and related subjects. I'd like to go to the A.C., too, but it doesn't give scholarships. My winning a scholarship to Jamestown College will enable the folks to send both Ethel and me there next fall. She does not know what career she wants. I want to be a journalist. That field is too crowded, but I can prepare for it with an English major and take enough side courses to teach school if nothing else.

The contractor, Jackson, is almost through with the north road. Old Hans told him one day, "De road all too narrow—not vide enough. All too low—not high enough."

"Well, b' gosh," says Jackson, "is it long enough?"

May 26, 1930, Monday
Graduation is over and we are home for the summer. I won two scholarships and will take the one at Jamestown. There were many compliments on my valedictory speech. Dad was beaming with pride. The speech was based on the class motto: "The one thing better than making a living is making a life."

It is doubtful the speech was really very good. What in billy-blue-blazes do I know about making a life?

May 30, 1930, Friday
Yesterday morning Theresa wanted the washing done, Ethel wanted the screens put on the windows, and I wanted the garden hoed. It was a busy morning. In the afternoon several schools were having an end-of-school picnic at Arrowwood Lake. Ethel and I wanted to go. Win came after her, but I couldn't go along because a heifer got into foxtail. The men were busy in the field, so I had to get her home and tied in a stall to lance her abscessed jaw.

June 1, 1930, Sunday

Yesterday Bud and I cultivated corn. The wind blew the whole oat field on us.

John and Theresa left today for good. We won't need them any more. Now that we girls are through high school Mama won't be staying in town in winter. Bud will get room and board there when the roads and weather are too bad for him to drive back and forth.

The wind and dirt are really moving. There is so much dirt in the air, even in the barn, one can't see clearly. A white setting hen in the barn is so dirty not a white feather shows. Dad's oats have already blown out, and the flax may go, too. My baby chickens are blowing to death. I've had to lock them in the calf shed for shelter.

Ted Roy told about the trouble he is having with his crop. He put it in and it blew out. He seeded again and it blew out. So he went fishing. His little daughter piped up, "And Mama cried."

June 9, 1930, Monday

Today was a typical day at Stony Brook—hot and windy. I got up at 5:00 and built a fire in the old coal range, carrying water and tending chickens while the stove got hot. Then I cooked breakfast, brought in the cows, milked them, did the separating, and tended the calves and hogs.

By the time the dishes and separator were washed, Ethel got up and helped wash clothes. Mama still has to take it easy after her operation. Dad told Ethel she must stay here this summer and help with the housework. That is a big boost. Since she kept the washing machine going during the time I was out hanging clothes and helped get the noon meal, the washing was done by noon.

Then in the afternoon I had time to do all the ironing, tend chickens, and check the cattle in the Big Pasture. By that time it was evening and all the morning chores to be repeated. Dad and Bud are busy from daylight till dark with the horses and field work.

June 18, 1930, Wednesday

The flax is nearly gone now—blown out. It is too bad. We really need the money that flax would have brought.

Mama is getting stronger, but the wind makes her very nervous. She has always hated the wind and tells that in California when she *was young she could put her hat on at a certain angle and it would stay that way all day. Dad says when he came here there was nothing to stop the wind between here and the North Pole. He broke its power some by putting up a barbed wire fence. He can always make Mama laugh.*

In spare time I'm breaking Pronto's three-year-old colt, Piute. Some people break horses in a rough way, but Dad taught Bud and me his way. Young horses are halter-broken and gentle at an early age. Draft horses are first worked between two older well-broken horses and not worked long enough at first to risk them getting sore shoulders. The saddle horses are accustomed to saddle and bridle before being mounted, and are so tame they are easy to handle. Of course, Pronto is something else, but she was broken before I got her. She's always hated men since she was broken, and she probably has good reason.

June 30, 1930, Monday
This afternoon I transplanted 70 cabbage plants from the hot bed to the garden and watered them. It is a long way from the well to carry all that water. Dad says he can't afford a pipe or hose to get water down there. Back in the good years, when he could have afforded it, God was providing enough rainfall and we didn't need it.

This morning we spent all morning getting the wash done.

Washing clothes in those days took a lot of time, even though, in more prosperous times, Dad had provided conveniences for the job which most farm households did not have. All farm women kept a barrel beneath a corner of the roof to catch rain water from the gutters. This soft water was used for shampoos and washing clothes. Instead of a barrel, Dad had a big concrete cistern to store rain water. A small hand pump brought the water right to the kitchen sink. Most of the water we used was hard water carried by pail from the well. Cistern water was for laundry. We filled a big copper boiler with pails of soft water and heated it on the coal range until the water boiled. Clothes were boiled for a few minutes, then fished out of the boiler with a long stick and transferred to the washing machine.

Most farm women had to scrub their clothes by hand on a washboard, but we had a wooden tub with an agitator inside, which we ran by pulling back and forth a handle on the side of the tub. We cranked a wringer by hand to rid the clothes of the soapy water as they went into the rinse water.

After the clothes were boiled, one of us would agitate them ten or fifteen minutes in the washing machine, then wring them into a tub of warm rinse water. We had filled the machine and that tub with warm water from the reservoir of the cookstove and kettles of water heated on top of the stove.

From the warm rinse we wrung the clothes into a tub of cold rinse filled with pails of water carried directly from the cistern pump, with bluing added to that rinse to whiten the clothes. Then we moved the wringer again to squeeze out the water and let the clothes drop into the clothes basket, which we carried to the clothesline west of the house. The ones to be starched we had dipped in and wrung out of a kettle of starch made by cooking some laundry starch in water (by then people could buy laundry starch instead of making it from potatoes).

In summer the clothes dried fast. In winter they froze and drying had to be finished in the house. If it was a windy day—as it nearly always was—Dad's bees in the hives west of the house were apt to attack us because the flapping sheets annoyed them.

When the washing was done, we emptied the machine and tubs and put them away, saving the soapy water for scrubbing floors. Making soap and carrying water were work—we did not waste soapy water. We did not waste any water, in fact, but used the rinse water on the plants.

As the clothes dried we carried them back to the house, folded and put away those not to be ironed, and dampened and rolled up the ones to be ironed. By the time the washing was done, the floors scrubbed, and the bread baked (usually we baked bread on wash day because the stove had to be kept hot anyway for the wash boiler), there was not often time to iron, so that was done the next day.

We had three sadirons and one handle to fit them all. As one cooled in use, we put it back on the stove and attached the handle to a hot one. The irons were heavy but not very big, so ironing took a lot of time in the days before some genius produced permanent press fabrics.

To make soap, we saved and strained all the grease from cooking. When enough was accumulated, we mixed it with lye and water in a big kettle to cook long and slowly, with frequent stirring, until it was of a jelly-like consistency. When it cooled enough, we poured it into shallow cardboard boxes to harden, cutting it into bars before it hardened too much.

July 10, 1930, Thursday
Dad has been at Commissioners' meeting most of the time since the first of the month. He hired a man to help Bud and me with the hay, but will fire him when he comes home tomorrow. We have to show some sense about the amount of work horses do in the field in this hot weather. The man, yesterday, overworked Mike when it was too hot for the big, energetic horse. There was nothing Bud and I could do to save him. We kept the flies off, kept cold cloths on his head, and stayed with him until he died so he would know he was loved and would not die alone.

July 14, 1930, Monday
Dad fired the man who killed Mike, and he and Bud and I finished the haying this weekend. Dad now has hired old John Siberry to run the binder during harvest and he and Bud and I will do the shocking.

There is still no rain, and today was just a scorcher. Dad, Mama, and Bud went to Jamestown this afternoon. Dad phoned back from somewhere that as they drove by the Big Pasture he noticed a cow and calf were separated, and I better get over there and do something about it. I made the mistake of taking Piute instead of Pronto, and Piute isn't trained for roping yet. The river separated the bewildered calf from its mother. That dumb cow refused to cross the river without being roped and dragged across. There was no reason; the river is low, but maybe she is terrified of mud. Between the untrained horse and ornery cow I had a devil of a time but finally made it all right without getting hurt.

That summer I occasionally went roller-skating or dancing with a boy named Vern who lived a few miles away. By the end of the summer I stopped seeing him because he was getting marriage ideas. Most of the summer was just plain hard work in blistering heat to do chores, weeding, canning vegetables, cultivating, shocking grain, haying, and working with beef cattle. Dad, Ted, and Grover had to sell some cattle in August, despite low prices, because the pasture was giving out.

One August day I drove Mama and Ethel to visit Aunt Nona. Uncle Amos had lost their farm at Pingree in March and had rented a place on the Pipestem River quite a way west of Pingree. The land was poor, the fences in terrible shape, and the house just awful. The floors were warped, sloping, and had big holes. The walls were in bad condition, the doors did not fit, the roof leaked, and a kitchen had been added on so sloppily there was a wide crack that admitted flies in summer and cold air in winter. The well produced only three and a half pails of water a day, so they had to haul water.

Nona said she was getting used to it. At first she was terribly lonely on that little place tucked back of a hill after living a half-mile from town with railroads on two sides of the place and a highway in front of it. When they first moved, she would walk up on the hill every day to look east and see cars on the highway or some sign of humans.

They were going to have to stay there over winter, though it would be miserably cold in that poorly built house. Nona said the house and well could be fixed for very little money, but Uncle Amos got only twenty dollars profit from 160 acres of wheat. What little they got for eggs, cream, and sheep barely paid living expenses. The sheep kept Nona on the run all the time because she couldn't buy sheep fencing.

August 7, 1930

Still hot weather. I spent most the afternoon picking chokecherries at the lake and toting them home on Piute. Dad is away. Ethel left this afternoon, telling Mama she and Milly Brewer were going swimming in the river.

Mama doesn't know the river is down to a little water over two feet of gooey mud. When evening came and Ethel didn't, Mama phoned Brewers. They hadn't seen her. Though neither Mama nor I said anything, we both knew she had gone to meet Win, and Mama told me to go find her.

I met her just west of Scotts', walking home, and helped her up on Piute behind me. She had a case for her swimsuit and a jar of water. As we rode along, she tried to pour the water over her head to convince Mama she had been swimming. Piute was surprised by this maneuver. She and Ethel came to the parting of the ways. As Ethel fell off, she reached for something to hang onto. Instead of grabbing the saddle or me, she grabbed my shirt. My shirt and I came to the parting of the ways, too. Ethel walked the rest of the way home, and Mama says she can't go swimming any more because she was gone so long.

In September, 1930, Ethel and I enrolled in Jamestown College, though she, still in love with Win, did not want to go. We roomed in Sanford dormitory in a room with a dresser, two straight-backed chairs, a table, and two cots. The dorm had strict rules about quiet hours, lights out, and students being in by seven-thirty week nights and by eleven on weekends. Since the professors were notoriously stingy with good grades, and students on scholarships had to have grades of at least 90 to keep the scholarships, I was thankful for quiet hours.

Though missing my horses and the Stony Brook country, I dearly loved college and enjoyed the professors, especially one English professor, Dr. Macefield.

At one point I told my diary,

Vern keeps writing sappy letters. He bores me. He should have it through his head by now I absolutely will not consider marrying him. If I ever marry, it will be a man with whom I think I can get someplace in this world.

By November, when Bud had to stay in Kensal because the snow was so deep, Dad had to hire a man to help with the work. Mama sent us three dollars, which she said must last us until Christmas for spending money.

My chum Edith wrote an indignant letter about a well-to-do bachelor who ran a mercantile store in Kensal which he had inherited from his father.

Herb is foreclosing on McKenzie, taking his machinery, horses, everything. McKenzie ran a store bill at Herb's—a lot more than he could pay. A firm in Valley City held a mortgage on Mc, so Herb went to Valley and bought it up, making Mc in debt to him $900.00. Now Herb is taking 20 milk cows, some fine horses, the threshing machine, racks, wagons, everything. Of course Herb should have his money. But as far as I'm concerned, Herb should not have let anyone run such a store bill. If he does, he should take the consequences instead of taking it out on a helpless old couple. I just don't see what the McKenzies will do.

I seem to recall that the McKenzies, left with nothing but a farm mortgaged to the hilt and no way of saving it or making a living at all, drifted down to Jamestown. They soon died, she broken-hearted over the loss of her nice home and he over the farm and his beloved horses. Many fine old people who had owned prosperous farms lost out in the drouth and depression and did not live to see better times.

In early December I told my diary,

Bud wrote that if we girls possess any money he wants us to get Christmas presents for him to give Mama and Dad. I've been hoarding the three dollars Mama gave us last month so Ethel and I can shop for Christmas, but it is not going to stretch as far as it needs to.

CHAPTER 4

The Wind Rises

1931 started out, as most years did, cold and snowy.

January 26, 1931, Monday
*Mama writes that Dad wanted to go to the Commissioners' state
convention in Dickinson but didn't have the money. He has no money
to pay Ethel's tuition next semester. There is a little wheat to sell, but
it won't go far the way prices are. She says I can't get new shoes.
Shucks! I need shoes badly. It's awful to be broke. I've been trying very
hard to find a part-time job, but jobs are scarcer than hens' teeth.*

*Today we had to write connotations for English. I wrote on sunrise in
the Stony Brook country, and Macefield gave me the highest mark
possible.*

January 29, 1931, Thursday
*Mama writes she knows we must be broke. Dad sold a big load of
wheat to pay our bills but had to add the cream check to it. Eggs are
15¢ a dozen. Dad sent me 50¢ to get new heels for my shoes.*

At semester break in February, Dad and I tried to figure out how
to manage. There was not enough money to keep us in college
another semester. Much as he hated to borrow money, he was
going to do it to enable us to continue our education. Though I
could get a stenographic job in Jamestown for the summer, we
rejected the idea because the pay would be too low. We would

be better off if I came home and milked cows and raised chickens and turkeys, mostly turkeys. They were worth five dollars apiece in the fall. As we had most of the feed needed, including lots of grasshoppers, the money was chiefly profit. We saved all the turkey eggs for hatching and always had more eggs than could be brooded by the turkey hens wanting to set. The extras we put under setting chicken hens and added the babies to the turkeys' own families. I told my diary:

Turkeys are a lot of darned hard work. They are as dumb as sheep and must be constantly watched lest they commit suicide in some stupid way. A lot of their feed is grasshoppers they catch in the fields and meadows. We have to keep them shut up in the mornings until the coyotes are through mousing in the meadows, and then run our legs off in the evenings getting them penned up before the coyotes are out again.

Dampness is death on young turkeys. They must be protected from dew and rain as well as from skunks, weasels, coyotes, and their own general stupidity. Ever since I started raising the feeble-minded creatures, they have kept Bud and me on the run. With Bud and me in school, the work of getting them hatched in the spring and ready for market in the fall will keep Dad and Mama on the run.

To pay Ethel's tuition and our room and board, Dad will have to borrow at least $200.00 this spring. He doesn't know how he will pay it back. We will have to hope for a good grain crop or better cattle prices. With luck, the turkeys should bring in about $750.00 next fall. There are going to be lots of places to put that money without trying to repay a debt and interest with some of it.

March of that year found me happy in my classes and happy because I got a job as a substitute in the college library. It paid twenty-five cents an hour. That bought a few things Ethel and I needed, such as hairpins, notebooks, and stockings.

We went home in early April for a brief Easter vacation. Writing of that I said,

I rode to Grandma's Saturday afternoon for a visit with her and Grover and Ted, as well as Piute. Grover's Brownie is lame, so he borrowed Piute to use this winter.

Going home I rode slowly, enjoying the familiar sights such as the muddy road through the flat, the view of Grandma's place cuddled in the hills, the brown Big Pasture hills, Pronto's long black mane blowing in the wind, cattle in the foothills, Mrs. Smith sweeping her doorstep, the ice-covered Big Spring and hills above it reflected in Stony Brook. I love that country.

Sunday I woke up real early and went out and milked, as the hired man is off on Sunday. When Dad and Bud got to the barn, Bud mentioned that the Easter rabbit had left on his dresser a big chocolate egg with his name on it in white frosting. Dad said it must have been the same rabbit who milked the cows before they got up.

I've applied for work in the library as a regular, not substitute, next year. Hilda says the Dean is very pleased with my work, and she thinks I'll get all I have time for next year.

April 10, 1931, Friday
Nancy said she heard Dr. Knight telling another prof about giving us a biology test on April Fool's Day and never looking at the papers. Today he happened to look at them. They all merely said "April Fool." Dr. K. thought that about the best joke ever.

We had narrations in English and were supposed to write 300 words about an incident in which a man ordered an elaborate meal in a restaurant and made a good impression on the waiter. When the check came he confessed he had not a cent in the world with which to pay it. At the end of class we read our narrations aloud. Frank had written a bit of elaboration on the above facts and concluded, "The other 189 words are what the waiter said."

April 26, 1931, Sunday
We had hoped to get a cream check from home yesterday, but didn't. We are destitute. So I am out of luck for a spring coat. Ethel and I owe five dollars for sorority dues. At 25¢ an hour for just substitute work in the library, it will be difficult to save up the five dollars.

May 14, 1931, Thursday
There is nothing going on today, so for a change I'll tell just how the day went. Got up at 5:20 and did some ironing and mending. Went to

breakfast at 7:15. We had cereal, toast and jam, and a cup of coffee.

Classes start at 8:00. As Freshmen, we are allowed only one elective subject. I chose French with the idea of majoring in English and minoring in languages. Our French prof is not a very good teacher.

Swimming classes are compulsory, as are physical ed, speech, Bible, English, and a science course.

Physical ed is a bore except when we play tennis. That is not always feasible in this climate. Bible and English are very interesting courses. I don't care anything about science and, being naturally lazy, took biology with the idea it would be the easiest.

After tennis, Bible, chapel, French class, and a study period, we had a lunch of soup, salad, a fried egg, half a slice of bread, and a glass of milk. After biology class I typed Bible notes. By 3:15, not having been called for library work and restless from staying indoors, I walked to the downtown library and browsed through it until dinner time. For dinner we had spare ribs and dressing, mashed potatoes, sauerkraut, and tapioca.

After dinner I finished my book reading assignment, finished typing Bible notes, wrote my theme for English, and mended stockings. It takes a lot of time to make ancient stockings look respectable.

May 25, 1931, Monday

We went home Friday evening. Saturday Dad plowed and Walt, the hired man, planted corn. Bud and I milked twelve cows. We have to break some heifers and have more milk this summer because cream checks are getting better.

Bud was breaking a heifer Saturday and spent more time dodging than milking. Once he came sailing out of the stall and said, "That cow may be a mother, but she's no lady!"

After chores I spent the morning and part of the afternoon washing clothes, cleaning, baking, and fussing with chickens. In the afternoon I checked the Big Pasture, then galloped home to do chores again. Just then Win and Lyle drove in, Win to take Ethel to the movie and dance in town and Lyle wanting to take me. I couldn't go. I was dust from head to foot. It would take too long to do the chores, bathe, shampoo, and dress. Obviously Lyle thought I didn't want to go. I wanted to, but GEE-EE-WHIZ!

June 8, 1931, Monday

Summer vacation has started, and fourteen cows to milk. Mama says I must take entire charge of the Big Pasture this summer. Grover and Ted keep cattle there, too, and have always helped with fence repair and checking cattle. Ted is not well enough and Grover too busy. Dr. Depuy told Dad last week that Ted will never be any better. He has not been strong since the flu epidemic of 1918, which apparently affected his heart. The whole family was so upset over Uncle Will's death in the epidemic that no one realized how sick Ted was.

It is so dry the fields are already brown, and Dad can't seed flax in the ground he has prepared for it. We are hauling water to the garden. Today Bud and I managed to get some hay in. Hay is scarce this year.

June 22, 1931, Monday

Rain! It began in the night and rained hard for a while. Dad has been seeding flax all day. It is a gamble, but profitable if he wins.

Dad, badly in need of another team of draft horses, got a team cheaply from Frank Gatlin. They are the most contrary pair I ever saw. Their names were Topsy and Daisy. Bud has renamed them Topsy and Turvy.

June 30, 1931, Tuesday

It is so hot! Dad's flax just cooked in the ground. It is all gone. Fields and pastures are burned brown.

The heat deaths in the country total 1,231. I mean humans. Lord only knows how many animals have died. Scotts recently lost their dog and a cow to the heat. Cattle are starving all over the state, and there is no market for them. Horses drop dead in the fields from the heat. The milk cows have so little to eat they are going dry. People pasture their grain fields and then plow them up to conserve moisture for next year—if moisture comes. This is our third year of drouth, and in a severe depression.

If good rains don't come soon, the Big Pasture will last only until August. Then the cattle must go to market or starve, and they are not worth shipping.

The turkeys have done fine, but it is so hot the hens I set for baby chicks have just quit setting. There are only 130 baby chicks.

This aftenoon, by the time I finished ironing, I had no pep left and lay on the bed in Bud's room watching Dad and Bud cultivate in the heat and dust. It made me cool to think how much hotter they were.

July 10, 1931, Friday
Dad is at Commissioners' meeting and will be for at least another week. I've been cultivating the garden and his shelterbelt. Today was so hot and windy I had a hard time hoeing the potatoes and riding to the Big Pasture to check cattle. Those jobs took all day except chore time.

On the way to the Big Pasture I found a meadowlark caught in the woven wire near Scott's place. Obviously I'd have to take it home and care for it for a while, so I left it with Mrs. Scott to be watered and cared for until I got back.

In one of the coulees was what the coyotes had left of a calf. The calves are weak. Their mothers are not getting enough grass to nurse them properly.

On the way home, when I stopped to pick up the meadowlark, Mrs. Scott's grandson petted Piute and then, holding up his fingers, declared she is dirty. I reckon so. Since she was born it has never rained enough to rinse the dust off her.

Tonight the wind has ceased and there is a beautiful opalescent sky.

During the next two weeks I got the peas canned—by hauling water to the garden every evening we got a fair vegetable crop—and Bud and I shocked the grain as Dad cut it. The crop was so poor the only tiring thing about shocking was walking from bundle to bundle. Except for Piute and the four horses needed to pull the binder, we had turned the horses out to fend for themselves as best they could because we had no pasture for them.

In the two weeks after that I found time to tell my diary a lot. There was no one to talk to about these things.

July 25, 1931, Saturday
This was a typical day. Up at 5:00 to go a mile for the cows and milk them. Fed and watered the chickens and turkeys. Separated the milk.

Fixed a pancake breakfast for the men and fed the hogs and calves. Washed the dishes and separator, baked and frosted a cake, and put a pudding in the oven. A bull got loose and was attacking the trees in Dad's shelterbelt. Got him back in and scraped the burned edges off the pudding. Rode Piute to the cornfield for Bud to use checking the yearlings. It isn't that Bud doesn't trust me, but he just feels better if he can ride over and check on the yearlings, especially his, himself. I understand. I cultivated corn while he did that and then rode Piute to the Big Pasture.

In the afteroon Mama wanted me to take her to town for a funeral. Ethel went along to go visiting. Mama says she is too old and nervous to drive the car, but it would be a big help if only Ethel would learn to drive. That trip to town took so long there wasn't time to weed the garden.

Nothing has been said—nothing ever is in this family—but I notice my witty, happy-hearted, fun-loving brother doesn't joke much lately. He is mourning about Isabelle.

Five years ago Dad started giving Bud his choice of one of the heifer calves each year, and has laughed that Bud always picks the best. The idea was to give Bud a start on his own herd of breeding stock, plus some steers to sell for college expenses.

Five years ago Bud picked the best calf and asked Dad, "Isn't she a good one?"

"She's a belle."

Bud threw his arms around the calf's neck and said, "Oh, you Isabelle!"

We don't name beef cattle or make pets of them. That one, however, was always called Isabelle and was Bud's pet.

Isabelle produced two good calves. Drouth, heat, and pasture shortages have been hard on the cattle. Whether that was the cause or not, I do not know, but Isabelle did not get with calf in time to calve last spring. She was due in late summer. Because she hadn't calved and seemed weak, we didn't take her to the Big Pasture. As time went on she weakened too much to graze or go to water here on the home place.

Bud and I did our best. We carried water and hay to her and went out with hand sickles to cut grass where we could find it so that she would have something green. When she refused even grain, I ground the grain in Mama's kitchen food grinder, soaked it with water, and made a mash she would nibble on.

Nothing worked. The day came when Isabelle could not eat or rise to her feet.

"Dad, is there anything you can do?"

"I'm sorry, Son."

There were no words or tears. Bud just went into the house and got his gun. Somehow, to me, the look on his face when he shot Isabelle stood for this whole tragedy of a land laid waste, a way of life destroyed, and a boy's long struggle ending in despair.

July 26, 1931, Sunday

Yesterday was so hot the men didn't go in the fields in the afternoon for fear of killing the horses. The thermometer registered 114°. Dad didn't believe it, so he put out another thermometer. It registered 116°. I picked and canned peas most of the day.

This evening Nona, Uncle Amos, and the kids drove in after spending a week in Minnesota. Uncle Amos's father is too old and unwell to manage his small dairy farm down near Minneapolis and has offered to deed it to them in exchange for giving him a home there as long as he lives. Nona doesn't want to move in with the grouchy old man, but they will have a decent house and maybe a better chance for the kids.

July 28, 1931, Tuesday

Yesterday I rode Piute to Grover's land at the lake to get chokecherries. We need all the wild fruit we can get. Though she is trained to stand when her reins are down, Piute left while I was picking because the flies tortured her so much. I slung the sack of cherries over my shoulder and started walking home. Grover was eating lunch down the hill and offered me some. I refused, but asked if he had seen a blazed-face bay mare who looked as if she were going places. He had caught her and put her in his barn. Wasn't that nice? I'd have had to walk a couple of miles home with 50 pounds of cherries.

August 1, 1931, Saturday

Wednesday I rounded up the horses and got them home. Thursday we rounded up the cattle to ship. It was raining that day, but too late to do the feed situation any good. In the morning we took all but the best breeding stock from the Big Pasture, then went south to get most of the yearlings.

It is a shame. Dad has been building up this herd for years and now is having to sell a lot of stock he depended on to carry on the herd. It will take years to build it up again. He won't get any price now. The bottom has dropped clear out of the market. There is just no feed in the country, and cattle are being shipped by the thousands.

When we got to the stockyards it was getting late. Dad rode on the freight train to South St. Paul. I had baked a lot of goodies for him to eat on the way.

Bud and I had to get home to do chores as soon as possible but couldn't hurry the tired horses too much. All the way home Bud sang "The Great Roundup":

When I think of the last great roundup
On the eve of eternity's dawn,
I think of the past of the cowboys
Who have been here with us and gone.

At home we turned the saddle horses, except Piute, out to rustle for a living again. Kiyo just howled and howled when they went. I know how he felt.

Bud was so tired that night he gave up on the particularly rambunctious heifer he is breaking to milk. He emerged from the stall dripping wet, said, "I may need a bath, but I don't like a milk bath," and turned the heifer out with her calf. Of course, in the morning he got her back to try again.

Edith sent a letter saying she is worn out shocking grain. "Say, isn't this a good joke?" she wrote. "My sister sent for a record and they were always out of stock. She sent to three companies for 'I Wish I Had a Talking Picture of You,' hers and her boy friend's favorite song. Finally she sent to Savage and got a package three days later. She was jumping around like a two-year-old before she opened it. Imagine her surprise when instead of 'Talking Picture' they sent 'She's Old and Bent but She Just Keeps Hoofin' Along.' They said they were out of the song ordered but were sending a similar one. Similar, huh?"

Yesterday, checking what cattle were left in the Big Pasture, I found a weak calf and could not find its mother—no dead cow, no childless cow. I dashed back for Bud to come over with a team and wagon to help load the calf to haul home. He said a certain beef heifer must be the mother. We walked through the cattle and found her, but she had a calf. The herd, scared of people on foot, ran for the hills. But first that heifer ran to the calf I had found, touched it with her nose, and then ran on with the other calf, leaving a bewildered little fellow behind. He was a twin, and his mother had taken the stronger calf! We took him home and will teach him to drink from a bucket until he is old enough for other feed. Teaching a calf to drink from a bucket is a messy job. Nature tells him nourishment comes from above, like manna from Heaven.

This afternoon I went to Grandma's to pick crabapples. She gave me some greening apples, too, "to make your father a pie when he comes home."

When it cooled down in the evening I got the milk cow Meekeye and calf home from the Big Pasture to wean the calf and add Meekeye to the milk cow herd. Lyle, watching from a hayfield where he was working late, thought it was quite a circus. The cow and calf would not stay together, and Pronto took the calf's dawdling as a personal affront. With ears laid back and teeth bared, she kept rushing after the calf and threatening mayhem.

August 6, 1931, Thursday
The first of the week Bud and I managed to get three loads of hay in the barn, picking it up in the meadow instead of stacking it out there. We also got the chicken houses and poultry pens cleaned again. Tuesday I met the train to bring Dad home. He got only $1312.00 for all those cattle.

Dad and Bud and I grieved over the sacrifice of the cattle, but at least we had some money and could manage for another year. Dad could pay back what he had borrowed and buy the year's supply of staples he bought every fall. Taxes and life insurance could be paid, and we could afford some clothes. Mama and I needed clothes; Dad had to have new boots, warm socks, and mittens; Bud needed everything. Not only were his old clothes threadbare, he had outgrown them. Bud's room and board during the winter months in town could be managed, as well as the twenty-five dollars a month it cost to have a hired man when Bud and I were gone. Ethel's tuition for the first semester could be paid, as well as our books (most of which we could share) and our room and board until Christmas, with a bit left over for emergencies.

There was enough hay, and probably enough grain, to feed what livestock we had left, but little, if any, grain to sell.

There would be only 125 turkeys to sell in November, but at five dollars apiece they would bring enough to pay most of the expenses until the next fall. My pay from library work would take care of little things Ethel and I would need.

Because the heat had discouraged the setting hens, there were no chickens to sell. There were enough to help out on the meat supply at home and bring in a little egg money. That, combined with cream checks, would pay for the few groceries needed after the staples were bought in the fall and also all the odds and ends from postage stamps to replacing a broken lamp chimney. Naturally, we were very careful of them in the daily chore of washing the chimneys of the kerosene lamps for the house and the lanterns we used in the barn after dark. It took five dozen eggs just to buy a new chimney. Not only did we have to wash the chimneys every day, we had to fill all the lamps and lanterns with kerosene and trim the wicks.

Just as we figured we could manage for another year, Ethel refused to go back to Jamestown College, saying she had decided to go to Ames, Iowa, and take up landscape architecture. Dad could not possibly afford to send her to an out-of-state college, so he offered to send her to the Agricultural College in Fargo. She would not go there, either, and stayed home.

In late August I wrote:

Yesterday checking the Big Pasture was depressing. The grass is brown. The cattle, seeking relief from flies, were on top of a bare hill facing the wind. Little calves were lying stretched out in the shade of their mothers.

Cousin Cora, Nona's oldest daughter, is here to have Mama make her school clothes. Though only eleven years old, she is a big help. She helped me pick wild plums to can and drove Jim and Jumbo, those huge horses, to save Bud and me time in gathering up hay.

September 5, 1931, Saturday

In the Big Pasture I found one of our milk cows has freshened and must be brought home for addition to the milk cow herd. Her calf is too weak to be driven the 2½ miles home. Besides, it was hot enough to wither a fence post. I rode to where Dad was mowing in the south meadow to tell him I needed help. He said since I have ascertained the cow is nursing the calf, we'll leave it until tomorrow and haul it home in a wagon.

Just then we noticed Mama out in the yard waving a dish towel—a sign to get home quick. I did. She sent me back to tell Dad the Kensal doctor wanted him on the phone. John Siberry was very sick, probably appendicitis, and must go to the hospital. Since he would be a welfare case, Dad must o.k. it. I galloped Piute back for Dad to use to get to the phone as fast as possible. Meanwhile I drove his team to mow hay and thought about John.

Everyone likes the old man, but no one knows much about him. Mama has feared something would happen to him and no one would know whom to notify. Even though it is bad form to ask questions about a man's past, she has tried, over a period of time, to learn about John. All she has found out is that he came originally from Ohio and has a brother there. For years John has lived in a little two-room shack on the main street of Kensal, using the front room as a shoe repair shop and living in the back room. The amount of work he gets mending shoes, boots, and harnesses must barely keep body and soul together because most people mend their own.

He evidently grew up on a farm and is good with horses and farm machinery. Dad sometimes hires him to drive horses in haying and harvest. He is too old and slow to get more than 50¢ a day, while a young, strong worker can get $1.00 a day. He probably doesn't average as much as 50¢ a day in town, and he likes to come out here. A change of scene, companionship, and home cooking count. He is very fond of one of the work teams, King and Daisy, especially Daisy, and is always bragging of what a smart horse she is.

One time he and Dad and I took King and Daisy to the Big Pasture to get a wagonload of firewood. When the horses got in the middle of

the river on the way home, Daisy, bothered by heat and flies, lay
down in the river.

"What do you think of your pet now?" Dad asked.

John declared, "I ain't proud of ye, Daisy. I ain't proud of ye a mite."

September 9, 1931, Wednesday

Yesterday Dad left for Commissioners' meeting early. As he was about
to leave, Central called to tell him word had come that John Siberry
had peritonitis and was very low.

Dad told Central he would get to Jamestown as fast as he could,
because John must not die alone, but Merritt, a good friend of John's,
could get there faster. He asked her to call Merritt. She had done so
just before calling Dad and could see Merritt leaving town at that
moment.

When Merritt got back to Kensal, he phoned to say John died
about three minutes before Dad got there and left no message.

September 12, 1931, Saturday

Thursday we went to John's funeral. It was an inexpensive funeral
because the county paid for it, but very nice. The minister gave a fine
service and many people came. Although there are not many flowers
this time of year and in this year of drouth, the women in town and
countryside cut all the flowers they had to cover the plain pine box in
which he was buried. All we will ever know about John is that he was
a nice old man we all liked.

Why did the county bury a penniless man like John, and why
did Dad have to approve his hospital bill? In those days welfare
was administered in each county by the Board of County
Commissioners. People were too proud to accept welfare if they
could help it. There was little waste or fraud because the
commissioners knew all the people and knew their needs. As the
Great Depression went on, so many people had to have help that
the counties and state went broke and the federal government
took over.

In that month of September, 1931, Aunt Nona, Uncle Amos,
and family moved to Minnesota to take over his father's farm.
Nona was never happy down there; each letter expressed a wish

to be back in Dakota. She never made it until she was buried at Pingree a few years later.

I enrolled in college again and gloated to my diary that by buying some secondhand books and sharing some with my roommate I managed to get $15.40 worth of books for $8.00 and sold two of my old books for enough to buy a pair of shoes.

Dad took me home most weekends in September and October to help gather in the potatoes and can chickens. I do not recall that we ever canned the stewing hens. As an old hen quit laying, we killed her for chicken pie or chicken and dumplings. In the fall we killed and canned the fryers we had not already eaten or sold. The steers and hogs were not butchered until cold weather. Livers, hearts, and tongues were eaten first. Dad made sausage and cured the bacon and hams. We canned the backbone and rib meat of the hogs and most of the meat from the steers. Canning meat enough to last a year was a lot of work. The invention of freezers has been a special blessing to farmers.

As Dad and I drove back and forth from Jamestown I told him any good and amusing stories of college activities—stories he would remember after I had forgotten them. He also would tell me stories of the days before I was born, and one day he mentioned that someone had become excited about treasure-hunting at Arrowwood Lake again. According to an old local legend, in the 1860s a party of miners going back to Iowa was surprised by hostile Indians while they camped at Arrowwood Lake. Only one escaped. He was said to have hidden most of the gold in a badger hole in a ravine and gone on home with the remainder in his pockets. He never returned. His son came years later and looked in vain for the gold. Dad said it was a good story, but he never saw a badger hole in a ravine.

If Dad had time when in Jamestown, he liked to call upon his old friend Archie McKecknie, and, because of my interest in history, would take me along if he could. Archie, who had immigrated from Scotland, had been sheriff of Dakota Territory in the 1870s. His domain ran from the Red River of the North as far west as there were white men in the Territory, north to the Canadian border, and south to the southern border of what is now South Dakota. In the 1930s he was a very old man confined to a wheelchair, but his mind and memory were good and he loved to have company.

One day when we went to his house we found another caller there, James Wheeler. He, too, had come to the Jamestown area before there was a Jamestown, in the 1870s. He had become very prosperous. He and his descendants were still prosperous, owning a lot of land and business interests.

Dad, Archie, and James got to talking about Limpy Jack Clayton, an outlaw who fled from lawmen all the way from Pennsylvania to Dakota Territory about 1870. The old Fort Totten Trail, between Fort Seward where Jamestown is now, and Fort Totten at Devils Lake, ran through what is now Dad's land. Limpy Jack established a dugout roadhouse along the trail. Remains of it can still be seen southwest of our house. There he entertained travelers along the trail and fleeced them in card games. Archie thought men had been murdered there. Dad said that in 1906 a hired man of his plowed up a human skull near the old dugout. It could not have been Limpy Jack's—he was reported to have been killed by a deputy sheriff in Bismarck in 1892.

James Wheeler told us, "Limpy Jack was a bad man—a very bad man. He stole horses and sold whisky to the Indians. A very bad man."

Just then his grandson drove up in a fancy Buick car to take him home. After they left, Archie settled back in his chair, relit his pipe, and said, "Limpy Jack was a baad mon—a verra baad mon. He stole horses. For every one he stole, Jim Wheeler stole a dozen. He sold whisky to the Indians. For every pint he sold, Jim Wheeler sold a gallon."

November 1, 1931, Sunday
Winter is coming. As I brought the cows in last night the sunset was a gold splash in the sky with cobwebs of southbound flights of ducks traced against it.

Dan is feeling discouraged. The price of butterfat has dropped 6¢ a pound. The price for No. 1 turkeys is only $4.00. That means $125.00 less in the money we had counted on to see us through until next fall.

*But the price of wheat is going up. Yesterday Dad went to Frank
Gatlin's to borrow some wagons for threshing. Frank, still in bed, stuck
his head out from under the covers and said, "Wheat sold at a dollar
a bushel in Chicago yesterday. I've got 2,500 bushels of wheat stored
on this place—and $11,000 worth of debts."*

He pulled the covers over his head again.

Farmers thought wheat at a dollar a bushel was a complete
disaster after World War I. If it was selling for one dollar a bushel
in Chicago in 1931, I'm sure it was not in Dakota. Though I've
found no record for 1931, wheat sold for thirty-six cents a bushel
in 1932 and rose to only fifty-three cents by 1938. Frank did not
live to see that. Not only did many of the older people not live to
see better times, some of the young ones didn't either. Frank died
of a heart attack at age thirty-six.

November 2, 1931, Monday

*Yesterday afternoon all our grain was threshed in a few hours. Roy
Baker ran his machine. Dad, Bud, and two other men pitched the
stacked grain into it.*

*What a contrast to the threshing days when I was a kid—the
huge, snorting machine, the 10 or 12 bundle teams pulling rattling
wagons at full speed, the piercing whistle for water, wagons heaped
with threshed grain being driven into the yard. Instead of an afternoon,
threshing lasted for days. Those days were the most exciting time of
year for us kids. Prices and crops will come back, but not threshing
days. New machines are on the market, the combines.*

*This year there was no flax harvest. All those acres and acres of
wheat went four bushels to the acre. That is seed for next year and a
little to sell, which is more than most people got. There are 75 bushels
of barley and 300 of oats. That should furnish feed for the winter and
some seed for next year.*

December 4, 1931, Friday

*Dad got me home for Thanksgiving in spite of heavy snow. The next
Sunday he tried to take Bud to town to get back to school. It had
snowed so much by then the roads were impassable, so Bud slung his*

suitcase over his shoulder and walked the seven miles.

Dad and I had to be in Jamestown Tuesday morning. The hired man drove us in the bobsled the seven cold miles to Kensal in time to flag down the Soo train at 5 o'clock in the morning. We got off at Wimbledon and waited an hour for the Midland Continental, composed of one odd-looking railroad car for passengers and freight and an engine which must have dated back to the Ark. The car had a few benches for passengers to sit on and an old coal heater Dad kept stoking to take the chill off. Along the track the section crews were shoveling snow so the train could go through. Anyway, we got to Jamestown in time for my classes and Dad's Commissioner meeting.

The Dean in charge of the library is trying to get the whole darned library re-cataloged. Now someone who donates to the library wants a list of every book sent to him at once. We gals who work there are on the run every minute.

Mama writes there is a lot of snow up home. Herb, the storekeeper who foreclosed on the McKenzies, lost his store by fire last week. That will doubtless put him out of business. I don't feel too bad. Maybe he should learn what it is like.

December 11, 1931, Friday
All this extra work at the library, much as I need the money, is putting me behind with my studies. Maybe I can catch up this weekend. Without all marks above 90, I'll lose my scholarship, and I can't possibly continue college without it. But I'm so tired all the time.

We got through the lists today, so maybe the library will get a big donation. The rich man who can afford to give it will never know what his unreasonable demand took out of the hides of some young girls struggling to get an education. We'd quit, but we need the money.

My friend Ruby, who also works in the library, needs it badly. She is here on a scholarship. Her father, who is well-off, is opposed to education for women and won't give her a cent. Her mother, though closely watched, sometimes manages to send Ruby a dollar or two. A cousin with a job sends her a little money. The rest she must make. An old lady downtown lets Ruby have a light-housekeeping room in payment for the work Ruby does for her. She cannot afford to supply food, so sometimes all Ruby has to eat is oatmeal. The 25¢ she makes for every hour of library work just doesn't go far enough, even though we girls trying to get through college have learned, if anything, how to make 25¢ go a long way.

December 21, 1931, Monday

I am home for Christmas vacation and have been listening with glee to Ethel's story. Herb hired her and Milly Brewer to help him for two days sorting things after the fire. He paid them $1.00 a day.

A few days before that, Win had come to see Ethel. He had had a row with his brothers and was also on the outs with his mother. He and Ethel had another bitter quarrel that day. The next day he caught a ride to the northern part of the state.

Somewhere north of Devils Lake he decided he loved her after all and started home on foot. He thought he might have to spend the night with the Indians because passersby, thinking he was one, didn't offer him a ride.

Finally he got to Devils Lake and, after a series of adventures, back to Carrington, where his brother-in-law Claude gave him a job in Claude's garage.

Last Wednesday he called Ethel long distance and thought he was talking to her when he was really talking to Mama. She finally got it through his head that Ethel was in Kensal working in Herb's store.

He tried to call the store. There was no phone. Soon some kid came to the store and told her to go to Central because she was wanted on long-distance phone. (Long-distance calls are made only in case of dire emergency.) Then Bud came dashing up from the schoolhouse to tell her there was a long-distance call. As she started uptown to Central, both Mrs. Schieb and Mrs. Clancy told her. As she passed the drugstore, Mrs. Dunnum told her, and at the next store Madge did. Kensal saw to it she got the message.

It was such a poor connection they had trouble understanding each other. She said she was in town with the Brewers, who were leaving at 3:00 P.M. She meant to wait for him, but he didn't understand that and thought she would go home if he was not there by 3:00. His car was not operable, so he borrowed a car at Claude's shop and set out. The car broke down. He went back to Carrington and borrowed an old Hudson and started for Edmunds over terrible roads. When he finally got to Edmunds, Herman Siebert came along hauling a trailer loaded with chickens behind his car. He, too, was headed for Kensal. He broke trail and then kept stopping to go back and help Win. That way they got as far east as George Brewer's, nearly ten miles from Kensal. There the trailer tipped over in a drift, and the chickens got out. They had to run them down all over Brewer's potato field.

To leave them chasing chickens and get back to Ethel—she thought Win was coming to Kensal, so she had Brewers leave without her. She stayed with Madge until 5:00. Since there was still no sign of Win, she caught a ride to within a mile and a half of home. Then she started walking even though not suitably dressed for walking in the winter twilight. Just then Aunt Lydia and Unk came along on their way to Grandma's and gave her a ride. As they got to where our half-mile driveway joins the country road, Win came out the driveway. Ethel insisted that Unk let her out of his car. She started walking home. Win turned around and followed her. They were both boiling mad. He demanded to know where she had been and with whom. He said he had been down to our place and Dad ordered him off. That was not so. That was merely the way he took it when he got stuck in our yard and Dad told the hired man to help him until he got out.

Ethel said she was freezing; he should let her in his car. Then he thought she had walked all the way and was terribly remorseful. She didn't tell him she had ridden all the way until just then.

Anyway, they've made up again.

CHAPTER 5

The Gale

In January of 1932 I reported nothing but work, cold, and lots of snow.

January 31, 1932, Sunday
This ends January, thank goodness. It has been a stormy month, and the dorm is miserably cold. February is a short month. Spring begins in March.

Nona wrote that it is also cold and snowy in Minnesota. Amos's father legally turned the farm over to them, but she wishes he had it back and she was home in Dakota.

February 9, 1932
We are still working very hard in the library. When Dad saw it, he said he wished he could spend a whole winter there. I'd rather never see it again. However, it pays about two-thirds of my expenses, and that is a help to Dad. Butterfat is down to 19¢ and eggs 9¢ a dozen.

I want to quit the library. The Dean drives us to death and is so crabby. Next year I'll try to get a light-housekeeping room downtown. A cheap one, and bringing part of my food from home, will make living costs less than at the dorm and commons. Maybe I can get by cheaply enough not to have to work. Maybe next year it will rain. Maybe next year I can raise more turkeys. Maybe next year there will somehow be more money. If there isn't, maybe I can get a part-time job downtown. *Anything would be better than the library. The Dean works us too hard.*

February 29, 1932, Monday
The roads were passable enough that Dad got me home over the weekend. Bud was home, too, and we had a lot of fun joshing each other. Ethel, since New Year's, is visiting at Aunt Alice's.

I've learned that by March 3 in the "Dryden to Pope" course I must read 2 long old-time plays and 2 contemporary, "Palomon and Arate" and the Preface, 75 pages of dramatic criticism, 120 pages of Pepys' Diary, attend 2 lectures, prepare for an exam, and write a 1,000-word paper. GEE-EE-WHIZ! Each prof thinks we have nothing to do but prepare for his particular course.

April 11, 1932, Monday
It is still chilly weather. I got $14.00 in library pay today and need it. Money is so scarce, and Dad has lots of bills to pay. Fat cows are bringing 2½¢ a pound, and canners 1¢. That means a 900-pound canner cow brings $9.00. Butterfat has dropped to 15¢ a lb., and eggs are 4¢ a dozen. We were horrified when they went down to 15¢ last year.

April 25, 1932, Monday
Friday, at the library, Hilda told me expenses will be cut some more and only three of us hired next year. The Dean told her I must be one of the three. Ixnay! Three of us can't do it in spare time. We are worked as hard as possible now. If there are to be only three next year, I know who isn't going to be among them.

Ethel tells me she and Win have busted up again, and it is final this time. It just might be. Though they have been quarreling and making up regularly for two years, this time they apparently had a real potato-warmer of a row, and she is looking for another boy friend.

I rode fence Saturday to see where repairs are needed. All these miles of fence can get to need a lot of fixing. It will be a long time before there is grass enough in the pastures for the stock.

Yesterday Dad and I came early to Jamestown to go to Elder's horse sale barn. We must have a good cow pony. Pronto's legs are no good any more and we can't afford to keep a useless horse. Piute is too slow and doesn't suit Dad at all. I hate it, but we'll have to trade them both to get the kind of horse we need and have no money to buy.

Our former neighbor, Ernest, is working for Elder breaking horses. He didn't show us any horses we wanted but told us they are bringing in a young strawberry roan gelding from Montana, half-broken, with the rest of his training to be left to the buyer. He has good potential as a cow pony and has run six miles with a heavy man on his back.

"Wait until you see that roan," Ernest advised me. "You'll want him."

April 28, 1932, Thursday

It is cold, and I've taken my winter coat home.

Tuesday, as we entered the "Dryden to Pope" class, we saw a sign on the blackboard in Professor Macefield's handwriting: "Freshman English students write a 500-word theme on 'The Procrastination of Youth!'"

"The day after his birthday, too," Frank mourned. "He was 26 yesterday."

May 7, 1932, Saturday

Today Elder's men picked up Piute and Pronto. I rode in the truck with them to a pasture near Spiritwood Lake where the roan was. They helped me catch him and I rode him the 18 miles home. He is a good horse.

This afternoon Dad and I took the cattle to the Big Pasture. The grass isn't ready, but all the feed at home is gone. Dad wants me to take them out weekends (the only time I'll be home) and herd them along the roadsides to help tide them along.

Ethel still hasn't made up with Win and has decided to try to get Lyle to be her escort for dances and roller-skating this summer. That is a good joke on me. Lyle has been asking me for dates for a long time, and I had decided on him as an escort this summer. Well, let her have him. Dick and Henry also ask me for dates, but they bore me. Ernest and Cap are a lot of fun. Maybe I'll date one or the other when I have time to rollerskate or dance.

May 30, 1932, Monday

Dad and Mama's old friends, Ed and Ada, visited us yesterday afternoon. Ed says he wanted more milk cows, but from fourteen

Guernsey cows he got only one heifer calf, and she died. He says he
will never be able to pay off the bills from his youngest daughter's
illness, which total $450.00. His oldest daughter's husband is out of
work. She will teach in a country school this year, and they will live
with Ed and Ada. Pearson, who is on the school board, is running for
county commissioner in Foster County. Ed told him if his daughter
didn't get that teaching job, he, Ed, would run for commissioner and
get most of the votes Pearson would get otherwise. She got the job.

Ed says he sold a 350-pound hog for $2.00. The next week Ada
bought enough canned ham to make two dozen sandwiches for a club
meeting, and it cost her 40¢.

A neighbor of his had sixty young hogs refused at the market
because they were too thin. He bought $50.00 worth of feed, fattened
them up, and took them back to market. He got $51.60.

June 14, 1932

The college year ended last Wednesday.

Friday a cloudburst washed out the flax. Darn it! Flax is a good
price and every year something happens to it.

Saturday evening Lyle asked me to go to the dance with him. I had
been on the run all day and was too tired. He took Ethel.

Monday Dad was out in the potato field knocking potato bugs off
the plants into a pail. He was going to kill them by pouring kerosene
over them. When a sudden hailstorm came up, he set the pail down
in the barnyard so he could help with the terrified horses. A horse
kicked the bucket over. Several thousand of Dad's little jewels went
back to the potato field.

June 22, 1932, Wednesday

Last week we took Ethel over to Aunt Alice's because she wants to
visit there. Uncle George says he bugs the potatoes twice a day but
has to kick the grasshoppers out of the way first. He says the Bakers
have lost 100 acres of corn to the grasshoppers and have quit
cultivating because they are tired of giving the hoppers a ride around
the field.

So far, this summer, we have been getting enough rain. Hills that
were bare at this time last year are green. This land was getting in
such shape you couldn't raise a row on it unless you came here mad.

Sunday Dad and Bud and I rode to the Big Pasture to check the stock. Dad had us go up on the highest hill, where that reticent man talked to us, pointing out the land he owns and the tracts he had hoped, and still hopes, to acquire. He spoke of how valuable this ranch and herd will be someday. When Bud was born, Dad was refused more life insurance and told he had a heart condition that could kill him at any time. Dad never says anything about his heart, or pays any attention to it, but it may have been in his mind last Sunday.

He said, "Bud, times are hard, and I may not live to get all the land we need or to build the herd we should have. But you will. I want you to know what I think should be done. And always remember, the main thing is to have control of the water."

Bud replied, "Dad, I've decided I don't want to go into the cattle business. I want to be a civil engineer."

We all sat silently for a long time, just looking over the country. I knew what Dad was thinking, what Bud was thinking, and what I was thinking. But no one in this family ever says anything.

Dad was seeing his hopes and dreams go down the drain. He is a far-seeing man, and he knows what this place and his mother's and Grover's can be in the future. But Ted, no matter how long he lives, will never again be able to do much. Grover, nearing age 40, has never married. Perhaps he never will. If Bud doesn't carry the place on, who is going to do it? All the years of hard work on the part of Grandpa and his children will be lost. On the other hand, Dad knows how it is. When he was young, he did not want to stay on the ranch. He had no choice.

I'm old enough to remember the good years. Bud isn't. All he can remember are things like the loss of Isabelle, the heat, the cold, the work, the drouth, the everlasting struggle to make enough money to live from year to year.

I can see Dad's point of view. There is a future here. But what can a woman do? Who will listen to her?

Dad sat for a long time looking over the land. Then he spoke, very slowly, "Well, Son, if that is what you want, just pick out your school. We'll educate you to be a civil engineer."

In 1932 the rains which had given us hope ceased entirely in mid-June. As the hot, dry summer wore on, and as Bud and I worked at cultivating and haying, I tried to persuade him that good times would come again and his cattle would be worth a lot. He had always hung onto his heifer calves, some by that time being cows who produced calves. Lack of feed had forced him to sell his steers for very little money. He was saving the money to get through high school if Dad could not make it possible, otherwise to give him a start in college.

Once in a while that summer I went dancing or roller-skating at the pavilion beside the lake with Ernest. Jamestown College students were not allowed to dance, but of course some of us did when away from Jamestown. There was little time for dating at college, and no college boy there in those days owned a car. If he had fifty cents to spare, he could walk downtown with his girlfriend and go to a movie.

When Elder could no longer pay him, Ernest lost his job breaking horses. Then he worked on his father's farm the rest of the summer and as separator man on a threshing crew. He was witty, a lot of fun, and we were really fond of each other, being the same kind of people who thought the same things were funny. However, we did not have much time together. We were both too busy.

August 2, 1932, Tuesday

It is still hot and dry. Bud and I have the oats shocked and have put up a fair amount of hay. This morning I got the ironing done early and went out to shock the Ceres wheat, a new variety supposed to be drouth resistant. Dad is trying it this year. The long beards of that wheat come above my gauntlets and tear my arms. Dad found me lying in the shade of a shock thinking unprintable things about Ceres. He went to shocking it, saying I'd look more useful if I'd take the cream to market. So I did.

This evening I picked chokecherries in the Big Pasture, starting home just at sunset. Ducks were feeding quietly along the river. Behind me the hills were turning lavender. In front of me the fields were a golden mist. My country.

August 24, 1932

Yesterday I let a pan of cookies burn while watching the threshers move into the oat field. Mama had a lot to say about what a help I am around the house when something is going on outdoors.

The threshers are already finished here, which is lucky because after more than two months of no rain, it rained today. Forty acres of oats went 30 bushels to the acre, and fifteen acres of it went 23. Ceres wheat was 17½ bushels per acre, and Quality wheat went 17.

I haven't seen Ernest this month because he has worked all month as a separator man. He works thirteen hours a day running that machine out in the heat, then late at night and early in the morning must grease the machine and lace the belts.

August 25, 1932, Thursday

Today, at the grain elevator in Kensal, Dad and I saw Merritt. They've foreclosed on his farm, but he still has his sheep. As we talked, we saw Bert drive in with a big load of wheat.

Merritt said, "Ann, you ought to set your cap for him. He's a nice fellow with a good farm and buildings—all clear of debt."

"Maybe that's a good idea. And maybe you are loco in the coco. I don't want a man who can't walk into the living room without giving a lifelike imitation of a truck driver falling over a pile of horseshoes in a blacksmith shop."

This evening, after the chores were done, I came out to find Bud's six feet, three inches of brawny manhood sprawled all over the back steps as he watched a glorious moon rise over the hills. He was humming "When the Moon Comes over the Mountain." That's a sign he is blue and lonesome. When he is happy he sings "Cut Down the Old Pine Tree."

Well, I reckon he is blue and lonesome. The only girl he has ever gone out with is his high school sweetheart, Margaret. She is a truly lovely girl. I doubt if he has had the time or opportunity to see her all summer. She graduated last spring and is in nurse's training at Trinity Hospital in Jamestown.

September 1, 1932, Monday

While riding horseback I met Bert on the road. He told me that after selling his crop he is still $20.00 in debt on his threshing bill. Wait till I see Merritt!!!

In September I started college again, rooming in light-housekeeping rooms downtown with three other college girls.

Ethel still insisted she would go nowhere to college but Ames, Iowa. Dad simply could not manage it without borrowing money again or mortgaging something, and that he would not do. So Ethel stayed home until October. Then one of the Johnson girls wrote that she could have a job down in Rochester as housekeeper in a doctor's home, a household of three adults and one child. The work would be mostly cooking, with some laundry and cleaning. Ethel knew how to do those things and would have all the conveniences of a city home with which to work. The pay was good. She was happy to go—we were all happy. By working there until the next fall Ethel could save almost all the money she would need for a year at Ames. By the time that year was over I would be through college and could help pay her way, although Bud would be ready for college by that time and there was apt to be a problem managing her out-of-state expenses and college for him, too.

October 17, 1932
Ethel writes she doesn't like it in Rochester and won't stay. Dad sent her money to come home, but is very disappointed. Wheat is down to 32¢ and barley is 1¢ a bushel. Cattle are not worth the expense of shipping them. And expenses go on.

This weekend I washed, ironed, cleaned the house, churned the butter, and baked and decorated a birthday cake for Mama. Sunday afternoon I had time to go horseback riding and rode over to the river just as Bud, who was hunting, was wondering how to get four dead ducks out of the river without wading in icy water.

"Ann, why don't you ride in and get those ducks?"

"Because Roany is no retriever."

I rode in, picked up the birds, and tied them decoratively around the saddle. Roany paid no heed until we got out of the river. Then he either smelled blood or saw, out of the corner of his eye, new decorations on his saddle. He snorted, leaped heavenward, and hastily departed in the general direction of Mexico. He would not stop running until every duck was shaken loose from its moorings.

As I rode back across the prairie, Bud was strolling along picking up his ducks and singing at the top of his lungs:

In his horse corral a'standin' alone
Was this old caballo, a strawberry roan.
His legs are all spavined, he's got pigeon toes,
Little pig eyes and a big Roman nose,
Little pin ears with a split at the tip,
And a big 44 brand upon his left hip.
He's ewe-necked and old with a long lower jaw.
I can see with one eye he's a reg'lar outlaw.
Oh, that strawberry roan—oh, that strawberry roan—

I can probably write a theme for Dr. Sinclair's class out of that incident. I'll copy a couple of my themes here before I lose them.

The Strawberry Roan
There is an old cowboy ballad called "The Strawberry Roan" about a horse whose color is that peculiar mixture of sorrel and white which results in a pinkish tint. That song has been my brother's favorite ever since I got a strawberry roan cow pony. From that pony the whole family—the whole neighborhood—has learned to expect nothing but the unexpected.

This past summer a young man named Arthur moved to a place about six miles from home to manage the ranch of his widowed sister. He was reported to be both wealthy and handsome. I told my brother I must meet this paragon. There was no opportunity until a few days ago. Then he drove in and told Bud he was looking for stray cattle but, unable to get into the hills by automobile, would have to go home and get a saddle horse. Bud offered him the use of Roany.

As Arthur rode away, Bud chanted:

Oh, I suppose
You're a bronc-bustin' man
By the looks of your clothes.
Oh, that strawberree-ee-ee roan!

"Now I can meet Arthur when he thanks me for the use of my horse," I rejoiced.

But when Arthur returned he spoke a moment with Bud and left abruptly. I ran out to tell Bud how disappointed I was.

"Yeh, he went home to fix that handsome face of his. He is lucky to be alive. He whacked that bronc with a quirt, and Roany wiped up a whole brush-covered hillside with him. His handsome face is all skinned. He has a red eye with purple trimmings."

Bud went about his work singing:

Oh, the man ain't dead
Nor the man ain't alive
Who can ride that bronc
When he takes a high dive.
Oh, that strawberree-ee-ee roan!

Another theme is:

Morning in the Stony Brook County
As the sun rises, the hills cast long shadows and the fog begins to disappear, still half concealing the horses and cattle grazing in the hills. A hunting coyote, surprised to find himself so close to the only house in the valley, skulks away to his den in the foothills. At the farm, chickens and turkeys gather at their feeding troughs. The cats come to the barn door, wash their faces, and hopefully watch the boy and girl who are milking a dozen cows. The only sounds are the drumming of milk into the pails and the plaintive cowboy ballad the boy is singing.

Suddenly, after a "crash bang," the girl hurriedly emerges from a stall and pours into the cat dish all the milk in her pail.

"That all you got?" inquires the boy. "Didn't the old cow give anything?"

"She did. Six quarts and one kick."

The boy lifts a kitten from his shoulder and gently tosses it over to the dish to have breakfast with the other cats. There is silence again except for the swish of milk into the rapidly filling pails.

Ethel changed her mind about coming home. She wrote me that when she threatened to quit, her employers raised her salary, hired more help for her, bought her some bookends and a table lamp, kept fresh flowers in her room, and gave her every evening off. She was having a lot of fun with the boy named Mike she met down there the previous summer, and had bought some gorgeous clothes and a permanent wave.

Ernest took me to the Armistice Day dance just before leaving to try to find work in California, then said good-by with some kind words about how much he thought of me and how he would miss me. "He says he will write," I noted in my diary, "but I doubt it. He says he will come back in the spring, but I doubt it."

Ernest did write regularly for some time—interesting letters describing his trip and his experiences in California. He drifted to Oregon, still looking for work, and on to Alaska. I never heard from him again and now know he died in Alaska many years ago.

By November, 1932, unable to find part-time work downtown, I was working in the college library again.

That November I told my diary,

Dad thinks the country is going completely to the dogs. Roosevelt has been elected President, prohibition is to be repealed, and Bill Langer is now elected Governor of North Dakota. The political career of Langer has been about as soothing to Dad's nerves as a keg of dishes rolling down the stairs, though he admits the man keeps life interesting in North Dakota.

Bill Langer was a complex and controversial character who did many unorthodox things as a lawyer, attorney general, and later governor of North Dakota. As governor he made enemies of President Roosevelt's friends Harold Ickes and Henry Wallace by criticizing the way they administered federal relief programs. Harry Hopkins fired him as head of the program in North Dakota, and Langer was indicted for conspiring to defraud the U.S. government by corrupt administration of the program on the state level. After three trials he was acquitted and elected governor again.

In 1940 Langer won a U.S. Senate seat, but his enemies petitioned the Senate not to seat him. Investigators plowed through

North Dakota for months digging up Langer's record for thirty years past. Among other things they found he had been arrested sixteen times but always cleared of the charges. After more than a year of investigation and debate, the Senate seated him. He kept being reelected until his death. History may not rate him as a great senator, but he did a lot of favors for North Dakotans because everyone in Washington, D.C., was afraid of his vitriolic tongue. Any constituent asking a favor got it.

What Dad thought of Langer as a senator I never knew. In the 1920s and 1930s they were always on opposite sides of the political fence. Dad, a stickler for propriety and law and order, was critical of Langer's shenanigans. But when Dad died, the most beautiful letter of condolence Mama received was from Senator Langer. There is, after all, a mutual respect between people who stick up for their beliefs.

December 18, 1932, Sunday
I went home on Thursday last week to help drive cattle to the stock-yards. Dad didn't get much for them. Well, we can only hope for the best. Maybe next year there will be a good crop and better prices.

December 27, 1932, Tuesday
Last week was a rush of school work, exams, and getting ready for Christmas.

Dr. Sinclair asked me to join Sigma Tau Delta, the honorary English society. That made me happy. I enjoy the students in that society. We can have a lot of fun and learn a lot.

My last theme for his writing course was:

Harvest Time at Stony Brook
After placing the last bundle of wheat in a shock, I straightened slowly and painfully and paused a minute to stare across the field. It shimmered in a temperature of 102 degrees. Heat waves danced above the grain. The bundles I was handling sent out heat waves, too, and the air was as hot and oppressive as a furnace. A cloud of dust arose behind the clattering binder drawn by four red-nostriled horses, their hides caked with sweat and dust. I pitied those horses; I pitied

myself. Nothing for us but heat and dust and work. What was the use of it all? Hating the sunbaked prairie, I forced my tired arms to lift another heavy bundle.

At sunset I left the field and stood at the side of the road enjoying a breath of cool breeze coming up from the south. Some tourists, seeing me there, stopped to ask directions.

"This is pretty country out here," the driver remarked.

I looked at the field behind me. The heat waves were gone and the grain stood in a golden bath of dying sunlight. Beyond the field long shadows striped the gold of the valley. Back of the valley loomed black hills with lavendar mists in their coulees. Beyond it all burned a sunset words cannot depict.

"Yes, it is beautiful."

Macefield's English exam was impossible to finish. As we got hungry for lunch, we left. As I, the last to go, was leaving, Macefield asked me what I thought of the exam. I told him it was a masterpiece. If he had asked what it was a masterpiece of, I'd have told him that, too.

Saturday I took the presents over to Grandma's and got theirs for us. Every Christmas Grandma makes lots of her special Christmas cookies for all of us, pfeffernusse and marzipan. Saturday she gave me her recipes. I was glad to get them, but a bit sad, too. Someday Grandma, who will be 76 in June, will not be here to make them. I hope I can carry on the tradition, and feel she hopes so, too.

Pfeffernusse
3 eggs, well beaten
1¼ pounds of brown sugar,
no more—no less
1 teaspoon baking powder
1½ teaspoons cinnamon
1 teaspoon cloves
1 teaspoon allspice
½ teaspoon nutmeg
Flour enough to make
a stiff dough.
Make dough into rolls
the size of a finger.
Slice. Bake and frost
with powdered sugar
frosting.

Marzipan

6 eggs, well beaten
3 cups white sugar
1 cup butter
1 cup finely chopped nuts
lemon flavoring

flour to make a stiff
dough. Roll dough
and cut out in animal,
tree, or any figures.
Bake and frost with
powdered sugar frosting.

Grandma gave me some evergreen branches the Fergusons at
Medora sent her. We didn't have a tree, as it would have cost 25¢, so
I made an arrangement of the branches in a pail and decorated it
with our old tinsel and ornaments.

Christmas the weather was mild. In the evening we went to town
to the church program.

December 29, 1932, Thursday

While waiting for Dad to make up his mind whether or not he is going
to Buchanan, I've been sitting here by the window crocheting dresser
scarf edging. If he goes, Mama wants to go along and I am to look
after Bud, who has the flu, and take the bread out of the oven when
it is done. If he doesn't go, I'll head somewhere on Roany.

Bud is getting better. He just came downstairs. Dad, mindful of the
death of his brother Will, has been predicting dire consequences if he
gets out of bed, so I told him, "If Dad sees you, you will get double
pneumonia and die immediately if not sooner."

He went on to the kitchen, complaining, "I wanted sweetbread for
dinner, and what I got wasn't sweetbread. You can't fool an old hand
like me. Where is the soda?"

Mama called from the living room, "What's the matter now?"

"Aw, Bud didn't get the meat he wanted for dinner and now he is
busy having indigestion."

Bud, gargling in the kitchen, snorted and swallowed the gargle.
Now he is upstairs singing at the top of his lungs:

I'm all through raisin' whoopee
I sat up then and swore,
Cuz I don't ever want to see
Little pink elephants anymore!

Yep, Bud is getting better.

He has been feeling bad because as punishment for missing a basketball practice the coach left him out of the Woodworth game before Christmas. The reason Bud missed was that Dad wasn't home and the hired man wouldn't climb the windmill. Bud had to repair it alone, at night, when the temperature was 12 below zero. He didn't explain to the coach, as he thought the man ought to know he would do the right thing. Explaining might have done no good. To the coach, basketball practice would probably seem more important than fixing the windmill to get the livestock water. City people have different priorities than we do.

CHAPTER 6

Windshaken

Before college started again in January, 1933, I got a week's work as a substitute for the English teacher in Kensal High School while she was sick with the flu. In those days teachers had to pay their substitutes out of their own pockets, paying, as I recall, about half the amount of their own salaries.

January 16, 1933, Monday
Last Saturday night I heard Bud come in from a basketball game and went downstairs to show him where the pie was. He was a mess of blood because his nose had been broken. I helped him wash up and bandage it, then fed him lemon pie.

"Now we better get to bed," I told him, "before the folks wake up and find out what's happened."

"How about us going out and making a nice snowman?"

I had to tell Dad first thing in the morning so that he would let Bud sleep. Dad was angry. He doesn't think much of basketball playing anyway. After Dad and I did the chores and I had fixed his breakfast, I amused myself that cold, stormy morning by trying a new recipe, a whipped cream cake, which was so popular it was half gone by noon.

The recipe is:

Whip one cup cream and beat in
two egg yolks until frothy.
Add one teaspoon vanilla and

one cup sugar and beat well.
Fold in one and one-half cups
flour sifted with three
teaspoons baking power and
one-half teaspoon salt.
Fold in beaten egg whites.

I did not say what temperature the oven should be as there
was no gauge on the old coal range. From experience, I could
stick my hand in the oven and judge whether the temperature
was right for cake, bread, pie, or whatever was to be baked.
Experience told how to fire it to keep it at that temperature.

February 2, 1933, Thursday
At the semester break I kept house while Mama spent a few days
visiting friends in Valley City.

Dad brought me back to college last Tuesday and picked up
Mama at the train. My schedule this semester is Rural Sociology,
Cicero, Education 10, and Victorian Poetry on Monday, Wednesday,
and Friday; U.S. History, Education 17, Bible, and Physical Ed. on
Tuesday and Thursday.

Since I haven't had any Latin for four years, the prof says I may
have a hard time with Cicero but thinks I'll make it o.k. Before the
French prof was fired I didn't get enough credits to teach it. Latin is
more commonly taught in high school anyway, and if I can get
enough Latin courses in the next year and a half, I can teach Latin
in addition to English, history, commercial subjects, and social
science. That will be helpful in getting a job.

Today I asked the postmaster for a 2¢ stamp.

Thinking I had forgotten that letters take 3¢ now, he asked, "And
what are you going to do with a 2¢ stamp?"

"Stick it beside the 1¢ stamp I already have."

March 7, 1933, Tuesday
The weather and roads were bad all during February, but I got
home last Friday night. Saturday I spent quite a bit of time
practicing taxidermy on a pigeon that had died. It turned out fairly
well.

Meanwhile Dad was driving the teams to town with a load of

wheat to sell in order to buy coal. President Roosevelt has declared a bank holiday. Dad couldn't sell the wheat and had to bring it back. He was really upset when he came into the house to break the sad news that evening.

I stopped winding the pigeon form and said, "Money is only a symbol, anyway."

He glared at me.

Mama, who was playing gin rummy with Bud, said, "Never mind, Dearie, you still have me."

He glared at her. "Damn it! You people don't take this seriously. I'm dead broke. We are nearly out of coal. And that damned Roosevelt has fixed it so I can't sell a load of wheat to buy coal!"

"Can we burn the wheat?" I asked.

I really wanted to know, but he glared at me again, so I said no more.

March 14, 1933, Tuesday
Though the roads are still bad, Bud is now driving back and forth to school so he can be home mornings and evenings to help Dad. Spring work will soon start, and Dad will need all the help he can get. He's been trying to get along without hiring any, but it is all too much for poor Dad.

Saturday I went riding in the hills. The rabbits are thick out there, playing games in the flats, bobbing over the hilltops ahead, scooting into the brush along the river banks, and sending the dog into ecstasies of hunting joy. The sky, between clouds, was that faint, delicate blue which is most pronounced in early spring.

Bud and I are tickled to death over an invitation from the Fergusons to visit them at Medora next summer. I've been trying to save a few dollars for the trip, which will probably cost about $10.00, but haven't saved nearly enough. I could get more work at the library, but don't have time. The Cicero course is rough.

March 30, 1933
Ethel wrote that she is sick. Her wisdom teeth are impacted. She had one out, and the other three must be extracted. Dad gave Bud all the money he had to drive down to Rochester and get her because she said she had no money for a train ticket.

April 6, 1933, Thursday

Ethel looks well, but her jaw is sore. I stayed home to do the work so Mama could devote her time to Ethel, but just had to get back for classes last Tuesday.

She has lots and lots of new clothes and got another permanent before coming home. Those things and the cost of pulling her tooth took all her money. She hasn't saved a cent for college next year. If her other wisdom teeth must come out, Dad will have to pay for that. I don't know how.

April 20, 1933, Thursday

Easter vacation started last Thursday. Friday I rode to Grandma's to visit with her and Grover. The hired man, Willie, is rejoicing at the passage of the beer bill. People can now buy 3% beer in North Dakota. Maybe that will put a crimp in the bootlegger business. Willie says the beer bill will give a lot of men jobs. Grover and I failed to convince him liquor may cost a lot of men their jobs.

As I rode home, with Roany jumping all the puddles, prairie chickens were booming out on the flat, and somewhere two coyotes yelped at each other. Flocks of white geese cut the air half a mile north. The evening was so beautiful it hurt. I don't get homesick for people, but do for spring in the Stony Brook country.

Saturday Bud was running the fanning mill to clean grain. I offered to take his place if he would shoot me a rabbit to practice taxidermy. Dad diplomatically suggested I settle for a gopher because Bud could get that quicker.

That afternoon Mama sent me to Scotts' to get some magazines. When I mounted Roany with them, and he found he was being used as a packhorse, he started to buck. He's not vicious—just bucks once in a while out of good spirits. I can ride him until he gets tired of cutting up. All would have been well if Cece, Mrs. Scott's son, had not butted in. Cece, like a noble hero, tried to come to the rescue. That upset Roany. He stood on his hind legs and wiped his front feet on Cece (who retreated precipitately), then whirled and started for home, bucking all the way. When I got off to hand Mama her magazines, she informed me Mrs. Scott had phoned her to come pick up the pieces.

"Your girl is going to get killed! That horse is doing his best to throw her!"

Mama merely murmured, *"Yes, he does that every once in a while."*

Mrs. Scott was flabbergasted at Mama's unconcern, but Mama is used to Roany and me.

Some of the relatives were coming for dinner Easter Sunday, so the evening before we were making preparations. Bud was washing dishes, I got a cake in the oven before starting to prepare my gopher skin, and Ethel was stuffing a turkey.

Suddenly Bud announced, *"Lyle is here."*

Ethel hadn't expected him. She swooped out of the kitchen, removing her apron with one hand and her wave combs with the other, and went out to his car.

Mama, working a jigsaw puzzle at the dining room table, called to me, *"Ann, you better finish stuffing that turkey."*

"I can't. I'm stuffing a gopher, and my hands are covered with arsenic."

So Bud had to finish the turkey. I told him first to look in the oven and see if the cake was done.

"How do I know if it's done?"

"Stick a knife in the middle and see if it comes out clean."

"If it comes out clean, I'll stick all the knives in."

April 26, 1933, Wednesday
Last weekend I went home and helped Mama with the spring housecleaning. She accidentally sat on the gopher I had mounted. That is that. Bud and I are kind of thin, but Mama and Ethel tend to be plump!

Dad, Bud, and I also rode Roany, Moonlight, and Dakota Belle all around the fences and fixed them where repairs were needed.

Moonlight and Roany behaved pretty well all day, and so did Belle except one time she had a chance to grab Dad's hat in her teeth and toss it to the wind.

May 12, 1933
This semester I signed up for a course in Rural Sociology with the idea I might learn something that would be useful in future rural

living. Can't say that I have and am not impressed with Dr. S. as a teacher. One day I said to one of the other girls I wasn't getting much out of the course. She said she wasn't either and had not expected to. When I asked why, then, she took it, she said it is a notoriously easy course. I guess that is why most of them took it. This morning, in that class of thirty members, Dr. S. asked how many of us expect to spend our lives in rural areas. I was the only one. I'm not seeing the country from a glorified viewpoint, either. The Lord knows I've tasted its hardships, hard work, poverty, loneliness, cold, heat, and inconvenience. But I love the Stony Brook area and want to live there. I can do some good there and make a worthwhile life for myself.

Bud graduated from high school at the end of May, winning a scholarship to Jamestown College which he could not use because J.C. had no engineering courses. He planned to go to the Agricultural College in Fargo in the fall.

I went to Bud's baccalaureate service and reported in my diary that after the class of 1933 had been assured the fate of the world rested upon their shoulders, we sang a closing hymn and went home.

Since I'd managed to save ten dollars for expenses to go to Medora and visit the Fergusons, Bud and I decided to go at the end of June when the work would be done enough to permit a little time off before haying started.

In 1902 Dad's younger sister Annette, whom we called Aunt Nettie, had married Fred Ferguson, the son of North Dakota pioneers. She and Fred had two children, Lee and Laura. After living on the old family homestead nearly thirty years, they bought the Rough Riders Hotel at Medora in the North Dakota Badlands. The historic and picturesque hotel was the focal point of the historic and picturesque town of Medora while the Fergusons ran it. Fred and Nettie were noted for their hospitality and fine cooking. The hotel was a homelike place, full of fun and informality, and with each room decorated wth Nettie's needlework and handmade rugs.

That June of 1933 the temperature was over 100° every day.

Dad said he did not see how the country could stand another crop failure.

In June I stopped seeing Henry, with whom I'd been going to the Saturday night dances for several weeks. He was persistent with ideas of marriage, saying he would wait any length of time if I was not ready to marry, but wanted my promise to marry him someday. The more I saw of Henry, the more I missed Ernest, who had never been mushy or talked of marriage. Even after I refused to go out with him any more, Henry was very persistent.

One Sunday night the young people in our neighborhood decided to go swimming at the lake and then, after dark, have a weenie and marshmallow roast. Milly Brewer's date was a man named Joe who didn't like Henry but wanted me to go. According to the custom of the time, I must have an escort. Joe arranged that I go with a farmer near Kensal whom we called Cap. Cap and I were acquainted, but I don't recall we had ever dated before. We did for years after that.

Knowing that Henry would be looking for me, I told Mama I wouldn't tell her where I was going so she could truthfully tell Henry she didn't know, even though my leaving with a swimming suit and towel made it evident to her.

We swam until dark, then built a fire to cook our supper. Seeing the headlights of a car approaching, we knew Henry was looking for me and had guessed where to look. Joe and I went back in the lake, where Henry couldn't see us in the darkness and would conclude that Milly was there with Cap. Sure enough, Henry drove up and asked for me. No one knew where I was. The wise guy guessed. He took off his pants, under which he had swimming trunks, and waded out into the lake with his flashlight. He didn't find me. Each time the light swung to where Joe and I were, we ducked under the water.

When Henry finally gave up and left, we had our weenie roast. Cap told me how discontented he was. He had wanted to go to California when Ernest and some others went the previous fall, but his father died about that time. He promised his stepmother he would stay and run the farm until his half-brother was old enough. It was obvious Cap would do the right thing, and also obvious he had a steep trail to climb.

We all had an enjoyable evening except Lyle, who had to stay home to grind sickles. The cutting bars of mowing machines were armed with triangular teeth (sickles) which had to be sharpened often. This was done on a grindstone, a circular stone mounted on an axle in a stand. A man sat on a seat attached to the stand and turned the stone by a foot pedal while he sharpened the sickles against it. A can of water with a small hole in it was fastened above the stone to drip water on it slowly during the process. I've forgotten how many sickles there were to a cutter bar, but it took quite a while to sharpen them all. Bud and I used to get terribly bored with the job, but took turns—one sharpening sickles and the other making jokes.

One day in late June, as I returned from checking the Big Pasture, a car passed me. It was Win and his mother, who had been with out-of-state relatives for a year. Win let out a war whoop when he saw me. When I had a chance to speak to him the next day, he told me that as they drove down the road he said to his mother, "Here's the Stony Brook country. It would look like home to me if I could see Ann riding the hills again." Then, over the next hill, he saw me loping along on Roany. That is when he let out the war whoop and told his mother, "I never saw that horse before, but Ann is riding the same old trails."

On Monday, June 26, Bud and I started our long-planned trip to Medora, accompanied by Ethel and our cousin Lisa.

June 30, 1933, Friday

Homeward bound, with Bud at the wheel, and I'll write about our trip on the way home. Monday we picked up Lisa in Pingree in the early afternoon, arriving in Bismarck at 7:00 P.M. We went to see the new capitol building being erected to replace the one that burned down. Two million dollars was appropriated for this one. It is 389 feet long and will be 19 stories high. It is claimed it will be built for less money and have more usable space than any other state capitol.

We rented a log tourist cabin near the river for $1.00 and there ate the supper we brought with us. Then we walked uptown to look around and bought grape pop. The pop gave Lisa a stomach ache, which she told us about until midnight. We girls slept on the bed and Bud on the floor. The bed was uncomfortable. Bud said the upper side of the floor was hard.

Tuesday morning we went up to the bridge. I just yelled the night before when I saw the Missouri for the first time. Such a big river! After breakfast we went to the Historical Society building and the Roosevelt cabin, Theodore Roosevelt's home when he ranched in the Badlands. From there we drove about 150 miles to Medora, oh-ing and ah-ing all the way in from Painted Canyon.

The country has green hills and valleys, but much of it is miles of forbidding bare buttes and weird rock formations. The name "mauvais terres," or badlands, was given the area by the early French explorers and all the early maps show it as "mauvaises terres pour traverser," bad lands to travel through.

I just loved the Badlands and the Rough Riders Hotel, where the Fergusons gave us a grand welcome.

Wednesday morning Uncle Fred took us south of town, past the King ranch, to the petrified forest. We climbed buttes and raved over every view. In the afternoon Cousin Lee took us north to Peaceful Valley. We sat on a sandstone butte while I asked Lee 1,000 questions about ranching in the Badlands.

Yesterday we explored Mrs. Foley's curio shop and the Chateau de Morés. Last winter I read all the material I could find in the library about the Badlands, Theodore Roosevelt's ranching days there, and the romantic story of the Marquis de Morés and Medora von Hoffman, whom he married.

In the afternoon Lee took us to Sentinel Butte, so called because Custer, on his way to the battle of the Little Big Horn, posted sentinels there. The view from the top is well worth the steep climb.

After supper we climbed the butte back of the hotel and sat looking over the country until dark. As the lights went on in town, violin music floated up from somewhere, and we could hear the beat of hooves as cowboys rode into town. A waning moon slipped down over the buttes, and from south of the Chateau a coyote mourned.

We left at nine this morning. Aunt Nettie packed a nice lunch to send with us. It is now after eight in the evening. I've been writing this off and on all day as the old Ford rattles along at a top speed of 35 miles an hour. We will be home in about three hours—and hungry.

The gas, Bismarck motel, breakfast and lunch Tuesday, and a snack for all four of us this afternoon took my whole $10.00, so supper must wait until we get home. I can't feel any enthusiasm as I think of all the washing, ironing, and baking to be done at home. Haying is starting, too.

July 5, 1933, Wednesday

It has been hot, with a scorching wind to add to the general misery. We started haying this week. I've been driving the stacker team. Topsy and Turvy are very hard to control, and the wind keeps blowing hay off the stack for me to fork back up.

Saturday, while I was checking the Big Pasture, Dad and a prospective cattle buyer drove over there. They couldn't get across the river to see the cattle, so Dad rode Roany across. Then I called him back so the cattle buyer could ride across. I called him back so I could ride across. When the men were through, we repeated the process. The buyer thought we had a good ferry boat.

Sunday Joe and Milly drove down to get Ethel and me to go juneberry picking with them. The work wasn't done, so I said I'd join them later. After finishing the dishes and baking, I set out on Roany. When I spotted Ethel, Milly, and Joe about 3½ miles west of home, I put Roany to a lope along the sidehill toward them. The reins were hanging over the saddlehorn because I had juneberries in one hand and was using the other hand to select the biggest ones to eat as I rode along.

"Good gosh, girl!" Joe said. "You give me the jitters the way you ride. You'll get killed someday!"

"That's what the neighbors have been predicting for years, but I'll probably die in bed of old age complications."

On the way home I met Kathleen out horseback riding. She told me Win got married Saturday to a girl he met while visiting out-of-state. That is that.

This is a fine evening in my Stony Brook country. The sunset has built temples in the clouds and faded out until one can see the stars. The turkeys are settled down, and the cattle are disappearing into the blurring hills. A cool breeze is drifting in. Sure, things are tough sometimes, but I love it here and always will.

August that year continued hot and dry, baking the crops to the point we could only salvage feed and seed. Bud and I spent most days trying to get enough hay put up, though I managed also to can a fair amount of vegetables for winter.

In late August, Ethel came home from Aunt Alice's, where she had been staying. Then she and Mama caught a ride with friends to visit Mama's sister and family in Montana.

September 14, 1933, Thursday
My chum Edith has been visiting me part of the time Mama and Ethel have been gone. We had a lot of work to do, but had fun, too, and Bud took us to a dance at the lake one night.

One day Grandma and Aunt Evalyn came over and brought us some pie apples. We had had nothing but lemon pie. Mama and Ethel don't like it. When they left, Dad bought two dozen lemons and told me he wanted plenty of lemon pie.

The kittens, all five of them, are nearly grown and have prodigious appetites. Bud and I feed them lots of milk. Tabby hunts for them continually. One morning we kept count of what they ate while we did chores. In addition to the milk, they ate three English sparrows and two gophers.

As Bud was about to water the horses I called, "Here she comes with a rat for them."

He turned Daisy loose. "Now we'll send 'em a horse."

When Mama and Ethel came home, reporting a fine time, they said Uncle Calvin had raised six thousand bushels of wheat out in the Judith Basin. He could send his son, Bud's age, to college that fall.

Bud, too, could manage to go, though he was short of the necessary money. He had tried to save all his cattle money, but some had gone for other things. Prices were so low that if he sold all the stock he had left, the money would not see him through one year. However, Dad said he could help with the initial costs of books and tuition. After that Bud would be able to get through the year on what he had saved.

Then, at the last minute, Ethel announced she had decided to go to the Agricultural College. Dad could not send both Bud and Ethel to college in addition to helping me finish at Jamestown College. He could manage Ethel's initial expenses if he did not have to pay Bud's. Then, if Bud stayed home and saved him the expense of a hired man, he could manage the rest of Ethel's expenses. So Ethel went to the A.C.

My diary reveals I resented Dad's decision. It did not seem fair to Bud, who had worked so hard and saved every penny he could. At the same time, though, I could see Dad's point of view. In his family the system had been that the older ones went to college first, and, as they finished and got jobs, they helped the younger ones. Dad counted on Ethel and me to help Bud through college. I had only a year to go, but she had dropped out for two years. He was eager to get her through and was very happy that she had finally chosen a school he could afford.

After college started that fall I went home every weekend for weeks to help Bud harvest potatoes and corn. We also did quite a bit of duck hunting. Mama canned many of the ducks for variety meat in winter and made pillows from the feathers.

October 3, 1933, Tuesday
I'm really struggling with Elegiac Poetry because I don't have the Latin background for such an advanced course. The things those old Romans said in their poetry would make one blush. American Literature is hard because Macefield assigns terrific lessons. Shannon protested she couldn't do so much because she is taking 18 hours and must sleep sometimes.

"When you signed up for the course you knew it was the most advanced course in this college. This is a college, not an amusement hall, and you are expected to work."

Then he told about Cotton Mather, who at age twenty was a college graduate, a preacher, knew several languages, and had written books.

Someone asked what he did in his spare time.

Shannon said, "I bet he went to the movies."

My old friend Audrey, who works for a lawyer downtown, and I have been having fun now that I'm in Jamestown again. We frequently get together for supper in either her light-housekeeping room or mine.

October 16, 1933
Bud came after me Friday saying he needed me home to help pick corn and to make him apple pie.

I also made a lot of cookies and sent a box of them to Ethel. She writes that she is not getting along very well at the A.C., but is having a lot of fun running around with a fellow named Grant.

October 25, 1933, Wednesday
Sunday was cold and windy. Bud and I got the yearlings home and cut out the ones to be sold. Then I went riding. Heading northwest, I saw dense smoke rolling over the hills. Roany ran three miles, getting to the fire first, with the whole neighborhood close behind. The fire was on state land, probably caused by a hunter's cigarette. The state land has not been grazed, and the dry grass on it is now like tinder. The fact that the wind died down is all that prevented it from hitting the farms to the south, taking our precious haystacks and Lord knows what else. We beat it out at the sides. At the front, as the wind died down, the county road stopped it.

Cece said someone should warn Hylands. Down in the hollow where they live they couldn't see the fire coming, and the smoke was blowing the other way. The fire would hit them if the men with wet gunny sacks couldn't beat it out before it reached the brush back of their house. I offered to go, as a car couldn't and a man on foot would be too slow.

Bud, who had driven the car there with a pile of wet sacks, told me afterward that a man who saw me galloping away yelled, "Call her back! No horse will go through that fire. She'll be thrown and have her neck broken or be suffocated!"

Cece told him, "Aw, don't worry. That there horse would go through Hell. And she'd ride him every step of the way."

There was no danger, really. The smoke wasn't too thick where we were and the fire line there was thin enough that Roany just jumped over it.

After the fire was out, Bud and I did chores and he brought me back to Jamestown.

At supper Saturday night Dad entertained Bud and me by telling of his adventures years ago when he and Colonel Dana Wright traced the Sibley Trail for the State Historical Society. General Sibley came through this area chasing Indians after the Sioux massacre in Minnesota in 1862. With the heat and general hardships, he had an awful time. When he got to the Badlands, he gave up, reporting to his superiors they ought not to disturb Indians in this country as it is a fit place for the red devils to live.

Well, I better get to work. Vergil to translate, as well as Elegiac Poetry, Prose Style to study, oodles of outside reading for American Literature, and stockings to mend. Despite honestly working at it, my mark is down to 90 in Bible.

In November my diary reported I was getting A's in prose style and did not know why because I had learned absolutely nothing in that course.

Cap took me to the Armistice Day dance one weekend when Dad had brought me home to help vaccinate the calves for blackleg. Of the dance I wrote, "Lyle and I danced every waltz together as each of us thinks the other is the best waltzer in the country. Cap, bless his heart, thinks a waltz is a hop and a skip and a twenty-five yard dash."

Christmas vacation was bitterly cold. I went nowhere except to ride the three-mile round trip to the mailbox each day, and wrote, "Nothing has happened around here except that the men, last night, tied a range-bred heifer in the barn for the first time. Today they repaired the barn. I bet the cats didn't get much sleep last night."

My remark about the cats referred to the fact that on cold winter nights the cats slept in the barn on the backs of the horses. Until Dad bought Jim and Jumbo, Daisy was the horse with the broadest back. Our old tomcat Toby staked out his claim on her back, and woe betide any other cat who approached his horse.

Daisy loved oats, which she would eat in big gulps, carefully keeping her head over the feed box to avoid wasting any. One fall Dad was short of oats, so he told Long, the hired man, to mix it with corn. The next day Long gave Daisy the mixture. As usual, she grabbed a big mouthful and started to chew. Then she looked around at Long, spit out the grain, and said, "Uh-huh-huh-huh!" Long laughed over that the rest of his life, claiming it was the funniest thing he ever saw.

CHAPTER 7

The Dust Storms

January of 1934 found me very busy, but happy. Ethel, who had broken up with Grant, was unhappy at the Agricultural College. Though Bud was always cheerful and full of jokes, he was really frustrated and unhappy on the farm and eager to get started in college. He wanted to marry Margaret someday, but with the waste of the current year, it would be 1938, at least, before he could graduate.

In February, for my last semester, I signed up for the easiest schedule I had ever taken—Vergil, philosophy, special methods, practice teaching, American literature, and art appreciation.

February 19, 1934, Monday
Practice teaching is fun. The only trouble is the school is so far downtown I can't run fast enough to avoid being late for American Lit, which is bad in a lecture course.

One of the assignments I gave was a list of questions for the kids to use to interview firemen. One girl got up and gravely told us the greatest risk in a fireman's life is the fireman's ball.

Something funny happened Friday. Maisie, a freshman who also has a light-housekeeping room where I live, does not get along well with Mrs. Hanson, the freshman English teacher, and never gets good marks on her themes. I've tried to help her and honestly feel she deserves better marks than she gets.

Everyone at this college knows Mrs. Hanson is pretty dumb. Everyone also knows that Dr. Sinclair, head of the English Department, is very well-educated, well-qualified, and hard to get good marks from. Just for the heck of it, I suggested to Maisie she pick out a theme on which he had given me an A, copy it, and hand it in as her own. She did. Mrs. Hanson picked it all to pieces with scathing criticism and a mark of D. Maisie was mad. She took my theme and her copy of it to her advisor and told him the whole story. He laughed and laughed, then promised to switch her to another section of English I.

That winter and spring all of us near-grads at Jamestown College were desperately applying for jobs. Those going into teaching were qualified to teach in high school but willing to take anything. As there were dozens of applications for every job, mostly from experienced teachers, it was obvious we inexperienced ones would have trouble getting experience. In late April I told my diary:

Professor Travis says my practice teaching supervisor gave me a high recommendation. That is nice. But nothing is much help for us inexperienced girls looking for jobs. My applications to schools having vacancies all come back "No vacancies," meaning they have hired someone else.

One afternoon, as my friend Audrey and I walked downtown, we saw her friend Steve looking at one of the new grain drills. The new ones had steel boxes and cost $350.

Steve remarked, "If I had the money to buy that, I'd quit farming."

I told Bud about it the next Saturday when we were cleaning the old grain drill. He agreed with Steve but wished we could have a steelbox drill because it would be so much easier to clean.

We spent that whole Saturday cleaning the grain drill and clipping the draft horses. They grew a heavy coat of hair to withstand the North Dakota winters and did not shed it in time to avoid being overheated when spring work began. We used hand

clippers—something like barber clippers but much larger—to clip
the shaggy coats of the horses before field work began.

April 25, 1934, Wednesday
*Last weekend was the worst dust storm we ever had. We've been
having quite a bit of blowing dirt every year since the drouth started,
not only here, but all over the Great Plains. Many days this spring the
air is just full of dirt coming, literally, for hundreds of miles. It sifts into
everything. After we wash the dishes and put them away, so much
dust sifts into the cupboards we must wash them again before the
next meal. Clothes in the closets are covered with dust.*

*Last weekend no one was taking an automobile out for fear of
ruining the motor. I rode Roany to Frank's place to return a gear. To
find my way I had to ride right beside the fence, scarcely able to see
from one fence post to the next.*

*Newspapers say the deaths of many babies and old people are
attributed to breathing in so much dirt.*

May 7, 1934, Monday
*The dirt is still blowing. Last weekend Bud and I helped with the cattle
and had fun gathering weeds. Weeds give us greens for salad long
before anything in the garden is ready. We use dandelions, lamb's
quarter, and sheep sorrel. I like sheep sorrel best. Also, the leaves of
sheep sorrel, pounded and boiled down to a paste, make a good salve.*

*Still no job. I'm trying to persuade Dad I should apply for rural
school #3 out here where we went to school. I don't see a chance of
getting a job in a high school when so many experienced teachers are
out of work.*

*He argues that the pay is only $60.00 a month out here, while
even in a grade school in town I might get $75.00. Extra expenses in
town would probably eat up that extra $15.00. Miss Eston, the
practice teaching supervisor, told me her salary has been cut to
$75.00 after all the years she has been teaching in Jamestown. She
wants to get married. School boards will not hire married women
teachers in these hard times because they have husbands to support
them. Her fiancé is the sole support of his widowed mother and can't
support a wife, too. So she is just stuck in her job, hoping she won't*

get another salary cut because she can scarcely live on what she makes and dress the way she is expected to.

Dad argues the patrons always stir up so much trouble for a teacher at #3 some teachers have quit in mid-term. The teacher is also the janitor, so the hours are long.

I figure I can handle the work, kids, and patrons. My argument is that by teaching here I can work for my room and board at home, would not need new clothes, and so could send most of my pay to Ethel and Bud.

In April, Ethel had quit college, saying she did not feel well.

May 21, 1934, Monday

Ethel has been having stomach trouble. Dad has been taking her to doctors though suspecting her trouble is the fact that she often goes on a diet that may affect her health. The local doctor said he thought it might be chronic appendicitis, so Mama took Ethel by train to Valley City last week to have a surgeon there remove her appendix.

Saturday Dad, Bud, and I planted an acre of potatoes. There was so much dirt in the air I couldn't see Bud only a few feet in front of me. Even the air in the house was just a haze. In the evening the wind died down, and Cap came to take me to the movie. We joked about how hard it is to get cleaned up enough to go anywhere.

The newspapers report that on May 10 there was such a strong wind the experts in Chicago estimated 12,000,000 tons of Plains soil was dumped on that city. By the next day the sun was obscured in Washington, D.C., and ships 300 miles out at sea reported dust settling on their decks.

Sunday the dust wasn't so bad. Dad and I drove cattle to the Big Pasture. Then I churned butter and baked a ham, bread, and cookies for the men, as no telling when Mama will be back.

May 30, 1934, Wednesday

Ethel got along fine, so Mama left her at the hospital and came to Jamestown by train Friday. Dad took us both home.

The mess was incredible! Dirt had blown into the house all week and lay inches deep on everything. Every towel and curtain was just black. There wasn't a clean dish or cooking utensil. There was no food.

Oh, there were eggs and milk and one loaf left of the bread I baked the weekend before. I looked in the cooler box down the well (our refrigerator) and found a little ham and butter. It was late, so Mama and I cooked some ham and eggs for the men's supper because that was all we could fix in a hurry. It turned out they had been living on ham and eggs for two days.

Mama was very tired. After she had fixed starter for bread, I insisted she go to bed and I'd do all the dishes.

Starter for bread was made from water in which potatoes had been boiled, two or three mashed potatoes, sugar, salt, and yeast. To make bread we used three quarts of this with flour and warm water added. We left one quart to continue the starter for next time. The previous weekend I had made so much bread it took all the starter and there had been no time to make more.

It took until 10 o'clock to wash all the dirty dishes. That's not wiping them—just washing them. The cupboards had to be washed out to have a clean place to put them.

Saturday was a busy day. Before starting breakfast I had to sweep and wash all the dirt off the kitchen and dining room floors, wash the stove, pancake griddle, and dining room table and chairs. There was cooking, baking, and churning to be done for those hungry men. Dad is 6 feet 4 inches tall, with a big frame. Bud is 6 feet 3 inches and almost as big-boned as Dad. We say feeding them is like filling a silo.

Mama couldn't make bread until I carried water to wash the bread mixer. I couldn't churn until the churn was washed and scalded. We just couldn't do anything until something was washed first. Every room had to have dirt almost shoveled out of it before we could wash floors and furniture.

We had no time to wash clothes, but it was necessary. I had to wash out the boiler, wash tubs, and the washing machine before we could use them. Then every towel, curtain, piece of bedding, and garment had to be taken outdoors to have as much dust as possible shaken out before washing. The cistern is dry, so I had to carry all the water we needed from the well.

That evening Cap came to take me to the movie, as usual. Ixnay.

I'm sorry I snapped at Cap. It isn't his fault, or anyone's fault, but I was tired and cross. Life in what the newspapers call "the Dust Bowl" is becoming a gritty nightmare.

As commencement of June 6 approached, there was still no job in sight. Much as I wanted to get away, it seemed best to apply for no. 3, the rural school a mile and a half from home. The folks needed me. I could work for my room and board at home and have no extra clothes expense. The $60.00 a month would stretch over a lot of bills.

The school board was glad to hire me. By 1934 a rural school teacher had to be better educated than formerly, but still needed only one year of college. Since I had four, the board thought that made me all the better teacher. They got stung. I was trained as a high school teacher and could teach upper grades but didn't know how to teach a first grader to read. The pay was actually $59.40, as 60¢ was taken out each month for retirement fund.

At home there was less work to do than usual. There had been no moisture since Easter. The crops which hadn't blown out had baked in the ground. There would be no grain to cut and shock. The garden never came up. There was no corn to cultivate; it had not come up either. The hay meadows were rapidly burning up in the hot sun.

But what would we live on? The poultry and cream checks would not be enough. The cattle were starving out. Dad and Grover had already shipped a carload for practically nothing, and more would have to go. We were pasturing them on what was left of the grain fields.

Dad's herd was being sacrificed for nothing. At a time of life when he should have been able to slow up, he was working harder than ever, getting less money than ever, and seeing his lifetime of work go down the drain.

Cap was feeling blue. He had the support of his stepmother and five half-sisters and -brothers as well as his father's debts to pay. He could clear up the debts if he could get just one good crop. He had promised his stepmother he would stay and run the farm until his oldest half-brother was old enough. When that time came, the brother married and moved away to a rented place elsewhere. So it was necessary to wait until the next brother was old enough.

In late June I wrote:

One of the kittens fell down the well this morning. Bud and I nearly broke our necks getting him out in time to save a funeral in the family.

This country doesn't look pretty any more; it is too barren. I'm herding the milk cows on what is left of the grain fields. We replanted the corn and garden. Dad has the best well in this vicinity. If it holds out, we can carry water to the garden. If it doesn't rain, the corn is out of luck.

County Commissioner election was last Tuesday. Bud laments that Dad is away so much on Commissioner business that a lot of work is thrown on Bud. He asked Mama if Dad's opponent has any sons.

"I believe so."

"Well, it will be a joke on them if he is elected."

Dad was overwhelmingly re-elected.

July 6, 1934, Friday

I am still herding cows, and it is awfully hot. Where they have eaten every weed and blade of grain, Bud is plowing so the ground will be softened to absorb rain (if it comes). He is very fed up and anxious to get away to school and fit himself for a job.

Poor Bud. He has worked so hard and saved so hard. He has done without nice clothes and never went to a dance or movie oftener than about once a year because he was saving every penny for college. He hoped his livestock would pay his way for four years. The price was so low he didn't sell any last year. This year they are worth less, and he absolutely must sell them because there is not enough feed for them and no money to buy feed. All the stock he has won't pay his way through one year of college.

Grover has already had to ship out more cattle. He wanted me to help him. Roany and I got to Grandma's by 4:30 A.M. We got the cattle to the stockyards in Pingree by 10:00. Then back to herd cows on the wheat field again.

July 9, 1934, Monday

Saturday night Cap and I went to the movie, Claudette Colbert in The Torch Singer. *Afterward he bought ice cream cones and we sat in the* car in front of the store eating them. He brought up the subject of marriage. I reminded him that he promised, if I would go out with him occasionally, he would not mention marriage. I also pointed out the impossibility. He has to run the farm until Sonny is old enough and then will have nothing to start out on his own. I have to work until Ethel gets through college and can help Bud, at least two years. If she doesn't help Bud, we are looking at four years. Though I didn't mention it, in four years Cap will be thirty-six years old. Forget it.

He insisted he wants to get married now. Then I turned shrewish and said I'd seen him leave a dance last year with Joan. If he wants a wife, she would doubtless marry him.

He said he did take her home from a dance once, but there is absolutely nothing between him and Joan and I know it—I am all he wants and I know it.

"Let's not quarrel," I murmured. "Things will work out somehow."

He leaned back against the car seat, saying somberly, "Oh, how I wish it would rain."

The light from the store window was on his face. He is really a handsome man, with a John Barrymore profile and thick wavy auburn hair. Suddenly I seemed to see what his face will be someday—a tombstone on which is written the epitaph of dead dreams. I shivered.

"Oh, Sweetheart, you are cold and have no wrap. I'll take you home."

I didn't tell him I wasn't shivering from cold.

July 14, 1934, Saturday

Dad has been at Commissioners' meeting all week. I'm still herding the milk cows wherever I can find something for them to eat. Bud is disgusted with the everlasting heat and work. The one bright spot is that the turkeys are doing well and are a good price this year. Then this morning a dumb turkey, though the water dishes were full, tried to drink at the horse trough, fell in, and drowned. I've been going around here ever since making up limericks about how stupid turkeys are and chanting them to Bud, who gets a big laugh out of them.

July 18, 1934, Wednesday

It is 104° in the shade. The grain fields are all eaten up, so I'm herding the cows along the ditches of the roads. The garden is burned up. We don't dare carry water to it because the well is going dry and we need all the water there is for us and the livestock. The river is dry. We have fenced a lane from the Big Pasture to the lake so the beef cattle will have access to water.

August 1, 1934, Wednesday

Everything is just the same—hot and dry. Lee came from Medora for a visit. It was so nice to see him. He wants me to go out there Christmas vacation.

The drouth and dust storms are something fierce. As far as one can see are brown pastures and fields which, in the wind, just rise up and fill the air with dirt. It tortures animals and humans, makes house-keeping an everlasting drudgery, and ruins machinery.

The crops are long since ruined. In the spring wheat section of the U.S., a crop of 12 million bushels is expected instead of the usual 170 million. We have had such drouth for five years all subsoil moisture is gone. Fifteen feet down the ground is dry as dust. Trees are dying by the thousands. Cattle and horses are dying, some from starvation and some from dirt they eat on the grass.

The government is buying cattle, paying $20.00 a head for cows and $4.00 for calves, and not buying enough to do much good.

In August, Dad and Bud and I managed to put up a little hay, working only in the mornings because the afternoons were so hot we feared killing the horses.

Bud was definitely going to start college in September. He sold all the livestock he had to pay for books, tuition, and a few clothes and got a job in Fargo to pay for his room and board.

Some of what Dad got for his cattle would get Ethel started at the Agricultural College again. That meant he could not pay for her operation of the previous May, but he figured that since I had a job I could pay for the operation piecemeal and also help pay Bud's and Ethel's expenses at the Agricultural College.

Then Ethel refused to go back there. She had decided on a course of study at Urbana, Illinois. Dad, desperate to get her through college, gave her all the money he got from the sale of the cattle, even what he was saving to pay taxes, for her new clothes, train fare, and initial expenses. I was to send her $50.00 a month.

I told Bud that out of the $9.40 a month that would be left there would not be a cent for him. He assured me that for one year, at least, he could manage. So in early September I started teaching at no. 3, Bud went to the Agricultural College, and Ethel to Urbana. The next week I noted in my diary:

Monday Mama got a letter from Ethel that nothing she has taken at J.C. or the A.C. will count at Urbana. She would have to go four full years there to graduate. Even she knows that is out of the question, so she is going to come back and enroll at the A.C. again. After the awful sacrifice to send her, Mama and Dad are very disappointed. Dad says I am to send her no money but give the $50.00 a month to him. He will send her money as she needs it and use the rest to pay the taxes and pay her hospital bill. He has never been able to pay a cent on that.

The Army Engineers, just as they did six years ago, are running surveys in the Big Pasture.

There have also been some men around here working for the Biological Survey. They say they want to buy up the land around Jim and Arrowwood Lakes for a game refuge. They want Dad's land up near the lake for $10.00 an acre. It cost him $20.00 an acre.

The country is overrun with surveyors these days. The Missouri River Diversion Project has three automobiles full of them running around. Others are here about this game refuge idea, and some on a shelterbelt project. The Missouri D.P. people are going to turn this area into a huge lake. The game refuge people are going to let it revert to the wild. The shelterbelt people intend to put in a lot of trees to keep the wind from doing damage to the farms the other two outfits intend to eliminate. The geodetic survey has built a tower on a hill south of us to flash lights all night long, though I don't know why.

GEE-EE-WHIZ! Each group is going contrary to the next. We seem to have a bunch of bureaucratic idiots running around at taxpayers' expense determined to ruin this area somehow.

Our bountiful and interfering government sometimes creates awful messes. When this region was opened to homesteaders, the government and railroads encouraged people to come in here for an almost free 160 acres. The broken lives and broken hearts that caused was criminal. People back East had no idea a 160-acre tract here does not make a viable farm.

Grandpa realized that. He started out with 480 acres and planned to get more. The drouth of the 1880's cost him his pre-emption and tree claim. The fire forced him to mortgage the remaining 160 acres. It was a man-killing struggle, but his family managed to hang on until the prosperous times after 1900.

Then during the war the government cried out for all the wheat it could get. People came in here, bought small farms on mortgages, and planted wheat on land which should never have been plowed. After the war, prices dropped drastically. These people have never been able to pay their mortgages. The government has never done a thing to protect them against the terrible gouging of the wheat and cattle markets and of the railroads.

Now another prolonged drouth has struck at a time the whole country is suffering a severe depression. Men like Dad and the Holmes brothers, who have been here a long time, who have plenty of land and no mortgages, have a chance to hang on until better times come again. Better times will come. Meanwhile the man on a mortgaged 160 acres is out of luck.

Since 1920, the newspapers say, 43,000 farmers in North Dakota have lost their land through mortgage foreclosures. Langer has been putting a stop to that. Here in this neighborhood the government can foil Langer and his moratorium on mortgages with the game refuge scheme, or any other that puts the land in the hands of the federal government. Dr. Depuy, whose father's old ranch has been nothing but a headache to him for years, and who doesn't need money, has sold the Depuy ranch to the government for only $10.00 per acre. Therefore the government thinks all this land can be bought for so little. Arnold Friedman made the mistake of selling a good, but unimproved, half section of pasture land for $10.00 per acre. That sets a value for all the Friedman land. The bank has sold George Brewer's farm to the government for the mortgage against it. George will get—or at least has been promised—one or two hundred dollars for moving expense. Langer can't stop that sort of thing.

A government acquisition agent named Woodger is running all around trying to buy all the land around the lakes and river at ridiculously low prices. When these monkeys get through monkeying with the Stony Brook country, I don't want to be around to see it. The people here have their backs to the wall, largely through government monkey business.

They can't get Dad. The experiences of his youth left him with a horror of mortgages. Dad, too, has his back to the wall, what with Mama's and Ethel's doctor and hospital bills and Ethel's expensive college ideas. I know it took every penny, and thing he borrowed on his life insurance, to send Ethel to Urbana, but he has not mortgaged his land.

Cap and I went to the show Saturday night, The Last Roundup. That might be an apt title for what is happening under our noses.

Last night was a vision of warm, misty moonlight. When I took the milk pails out I stood in front of the house a few minutes drinking in the beauty until Mama came out and snapped, "Have you nothing to do but stand there and dream?"

"Nope, except milk nine cows, separate the milk, feed and water nine calves and twelve horses, shut the poultry in and fill their water dishes," says I, making tracks for the barn.

School takes up much of my time. It is cold for September, so I have to be there by 7:30 in the morning to fire the old stove and get the room warm enough for the kids. There are 22 classes a day and all janitor work, which takes anywhere from 5:15 until 6:00. I walk the mile and a half to school because there is no place to keep Roany during the day.

Some of the girls I graduated with don't have it that easy. Leona is really out in the sticks and has to ride horseback four miles to school. Grace has far more pupils than I do and gets only $50.00 a month.

Ethel came home the end of September and said she could not get any course she wanted at the Agricultural College and so was enrolling in the Valley City Normal School.

Back in the boom days North Dakota built six normal schools. That was too many—just as there had been too many towns, stores, churches, newspapers, and banks. In the 1930s the state had too many normal schools for the population and not enough money to staff and equip them properly. At that time the normal schools rated low scholastically and offered very limited courses. The folks could not understand why Ethel would choose such a school over the Agricultural College or other North Dakota colleges.

October 1, 1934, Monday

Woodger, the federal acquisition agent, finally got around to see Dad last Saturday. From the kitchen I could hear the whole conversation, and it amused me. Dad was sitting on the back steps, resting after the noon meal, when a government car drove up. In this country, when anyone drives in, you meet him at the gate with hand outstretched, making him welcome. Dad knew this was the agent who had been dealing with the banks to rob our neighbors of their land. He didn't get up.

Woodger, a small man with a toothbrush-shaped mustache, walked up to the steps and introduced himself. He told about the proposed refuge and said he was there to appraise Dad's land and make an offer for it.

"It is not for sale."

In a sneering and condescending tone, "Oh, I believe this whole area is. All your neighbors are selling."

"No, they aren't. The banks are selling their places from under them. This place is not mortgaged."

Woodger spoke of what a great benefit this wildlife refuge will be—something for the good of all the people.

"I didn't build this ranch up for the benefit of all the people, but for me and my family."

Woodger pulled out every argument he could think of, then finally said, "After all, this is submarginal land on which you can't make a living."

That was news to Dad. He stood up, very slowly. The little pipsqueak agent stared in amazement as the bulk of Dad loomed above him. Dad is six feet four inches in his stocking feet, and higher with his boots on. He weighs 250 pounds, mostly bone and muscle. He is so big-boned and broad-shouldered it takes 250 pounds to flesh him out properly. Because his face has kept firm flesh and his hair has stayed jet black, he looks far younger than he is. His blue eyes, startling in his swarthy face, have never lost their keenness. By the time he had drawn himself up to his full height, the agent was open-mouthed.

"Young man, I want to tell you something. I've been here since the Territorial days. I started out with the clothes on my back and a $10.00 gold piece. I was young and dumb and uneducated. I didn't know I couldn't make a living here, and I didn't have any government expert to tell me so.

"Young man, I've been fighting drouth and depression and blizzard and blackleg ever since the Territorial days. Everything you can see from here to the horizon belongs to me—the land, cattle, buildings, horses, and machinery. It is too late for you to tell me I can't make a living here. You better go away before you make me mad."

As Woodger scuttled for his car, Dad called after him, "By the way, when you get back to Washington, D.C., you can tell Franklin Delano Roosevelt I still have that $10.00 gold piece, too!"

Having gold is illegal now.

If Dad can get a decent price, he probably ought to sell. He is getting too old for a spread like this. Bud doesn't want it. Mama doesn't like it here. I love it, but am not going to. Everything I loved will be gone.

School was going well, with no discipline problems, but there were other problems.

An only child named Leo had just entered school at the age of eight. He did not want to go and had never before done anything he did not want to do. So, though not dumb, he refused to learn. It took about a month to teach him to write the letter *a*. Then I had him trace *b* until sure he knew it. But he wrote *8*.

"That won't do, Leo. You must write it the way other people do."

"This is the way *I'm* going to write it."

No matter what I said, that is the way he wrote it.

Finally he got down to *h*. One day he kept interrupting a class I was conducting to say he could not copy the *f* in the penmanship book. I knew he had done it many times; he just wanted attention. I told Carl to take Leo to the blackboard in the back of the room and show him how to write *f* and told Leo to be sure to watch while Carl showed him. A little later I glanced back there to see Carl had Leo by the nape of the neck and was rubbing his nose on the letter Leo had refused to look at. Probably Carl had the right idea of how to teach Leo.

All the other children did well except Dora, who had never passed a grade. After two years in one, she was simply pushed into the next. Her problem was probably correctible, but she had never had medical care. In her case, I found something she could learn. She showed interest one noon hour in a decoration for the school window I was crocheting from red string. I showed her how to make the stitches. Though she never learned to read instructions, she could copy any pattern I made and gave her. Under state law I had to try to teach her things she could not learn. There was no law against teaching her the needlework she could learn, and I've heard she became quite noted for her needlework and other handicrafts.

As cold weather came, I cobbled up a sand table to amuse the children at recess and noon hour. They had a good time making things from material we all brought from home—old pasteboard boxes, empty spools, wire, beads, and scraps of cloth.

The school board, hard up for money, gave me absolutely nothing but my salary and coal. The books were ancient, including geography books outdated by World War I. I had to keep drawing new countries, such as Czechoslovakia and Yugoslavia, on our maps and explaining that Constantinople had become Istanbul. The history books were dull and poorly written. It was hard to make the subject interesting to the pupils or convince them they were living in what would become history. I didn't know how, any more than I knew how to convince Leo that doing construction work did not mean emptying his paste jar over Carl's head.

October 13, 1934, Saturday
Woodger came again, claiming to have four thousand acres signed up. He offered Dad $17.00 an acre. That is ridiculous. For far inferior places they are having to pay the banks more than that to buy up the mortgages. He also called on Grandma one day. Grover and Ted would not have let him bother her, but they were out in the fields. As

soon as Grandma found out what he wanted, she just switched off her hearing aid.

The Scotts' land is being sold from under them, and Woodger would offer nothing at all for the buildings, saying they can be moved. How stupid! The strawshed barn, the garage, and the stone chicken coop can't possibly be moved. That leaves only the four-room house.

"And where the hell would I put it?" snorts Bill. "On my back?"

The farmers here haven't made anything for years. Most of them want to sell, but they must sell, not give it away. Ridens were offered only $2,000.00 for their farm, and they owe that much on it.

Bud writes that he likes school but misses me and Roany and Moonlight. "Give me a little outdoor work to this grind. Once in a while I get the idea that you and me and Roany and Moonlight ought to run about 100 head of them thar critters out to Medora and start in!"

Bud was not meant to be cooped up in a city. If, in addition to an engineering career, he could have a small ranch somewhere to get away from it all, it would be ideal for him.

October 31, 1934, Wednesday
We had a fun time at school today with a Hallowe'en party, and most of the parents came.

Dora is going like a house afire with her crocheting. She has just string to work with. If I ever get a few pennies ahead, I'll buy her some crochet thread. Right now there are no pennies to spare. Ethel's college expenses have taken all my money except what I gave Dad to pay taxes. Out of the next check I want to pay $30.00 for a $1,000.00 life insurance premium. Then if anything happens to me the folks will have the money to plant me and help Bud and Ethel to the extent I could if alive. That can be spared from the next check because poultry money will be coming in. In December I need to save a few dollars for Christmas presents, Christmas treats for my pupils, and a couple of dollars for bus fare to Medora. Yep, it will be a while before I can afford crochet thread for Dora.

November 7, 1934, Wednesday
Woodger came back and offered Dad $21.00 an acre. No dice. However, it is looking as if we will have to go. Dad and his mother and

brothers are the only ones who haven't sold. The government can condemn their land. This school no. 3 is doomed. It won't be able to open next year.

Dad has never seemed to regard the Badlands very highly. Now he says if he were twenty years younger, or I were a boy, he would take the Herefords out there under the new system of regulated grazing. Dad's age and rheumatism would keep him from the necessary hard riding in that perpendicular country, and I don't have the strength to do it all.

November 27, 1934, Tuesday

I'm worried. Friday Grover came over in the early evening to get me to help him with his cattle. When we finished, he talked a long time about this land acquisition program. The government has most of the land around here now by buying up mortgages and buying from people like Dr. Depuy of Jamestown, who was anxious to unload his father's old ranch and sold it for only $10 an acre. Now that all this has been accomplished and so much of the land needed for that game refuge acquired, the people who have held out for a fair price will have their land condemned. They don't even have money to hire lawyers to help fight for a fair deal.

For years Grover has been building up his own ranch on land he bought at Arrowwood Lake, a place he calls Pelican Roost. He is offered $15 an acre for it. He paid $25 and hasn't been able to pay it all off. He will come out of the deal in debt for land he no longer has.

The government wastes millions of dollars every year. It pays a guy like Woodger a fancy salary to cheat hard-working farmers out of their land. Grover will be forced to sell, at a serious loss, a ranch he has given the best years of his life to build up. Pelican Roost is the best-located place in this part of North Dakota, with good farm land, good hay land, plenty of trees, good water, and a mile of lakeshore. Places like that are hard to find. The land is essential, obviously, to the wildlife refuge if the silly thing is to be put in here. Instead of offering a fair price, Woodger is trying to get it for a fraction of its value.

December 3, 1934, Monday

It is six below zero today. That temperature speeded my mile and a half walk to the schoolhouse and speeded the process of making a fire. Last week all schools were closed Thursday and Friday for the Thanksgiving vacation.

I knew Bud had no money to spare for train fare home, but had hoped he could get a ride. He couldn't.

Dad and I can't manage all the work, especially days of Commissioners' meeting when he leaves so early and gets home so late. Sometimes weather or road conditions force him to stay in Jamestown overnight. Now that the daylight hours are so short, I'm gone from before daylight until after dark on schooldays. So Dad has hired an old man named Joe, who is very good with animals, to help. Joe is too old and stiff with rheumatism to do heavy work. For instance, he cannot haul in hay from the stacks. Dad and I can do that weekends. Dad always keeps plenty of hay in the mow. Joe can shove it down to the cattle and horses from there. He can milk the cows, tend poultry, and see to it the livestock has water available. The poor old man is all alone in the world. His wife died many years ago; he lost his farm in the 1920s. There is nothing for him but work until he dies or goes to the Poor Farm. Dad can pay him very little, but he is satisfied to have enough money for clothes and tobacco and is glad to be where he gets good food and a warm place to sleep.

Joe has been carrying a potato in his pocket, saying when the potato petrified it would be because his rheumatism had gone into the potato. Well, the potato petrified and Joe still has rheumatism. Dad says the smell of Joe's old pipe petrified the potato.

Between Christmas and New Year's I had three wonderful days with the Fergusons in Medora. As I got off the bus there at six o'clock in the morning, a woman sitting behind me said, "My God, is that girl getting off here?"

I helped around the hotel because some of the employees were on vacation, skated on the river, went to a dance, went hiking, and for a drive with Lee.

I met and had interesting visits with a man named Ben Bird. He was born in Dennison, Texas, in 1865 and started trailing Texas cattle to Montana in 1884 for the N-N outfit. He continued with the trail drives until 1892, when his last drive was with cattle for the Diamond C Ranch in the Killdeer Mountains of North Dakota.

The Dust Storms

He stayed in North Dakota as a horse breeder and seller and moved to Medora in 1926. He gave me a fine collection of rodeo pictures taken when he ran the Heart River Rodeo.

CHAPTER 8

Windswept

January 11, 1935, Friday
School started Monday. It is still vacation to me because Leo has been out with a bad cold all week. I've been getting exams ready, report cards, monthly reports, and all such stuff.

January 25, 1935, Friday
It is cold, 20° to 30° below every day, and I haven't been off the place for two weeks except to walk to the schoolhouse and back, wearing all the clothes I own to keep warm. One morning it was 23° below inside the old schoolhouse. It takes two hours to warm up the room for the kids, and even then I have to keep them all near the stove.

Last weekend, when it was very cold and stormy, a salesman going from Minot to Fargo got his car stuck while trying to cut across to Highway #9 by way of the road north of our place. He followed the fence through the storm until he got to our barn and asked Dad to pull him out with a team of horses. Dad agreed to, but urged him to go to the house first to warm up and have dinner.

"Go right up to the house and make yourself at home," Dad said. "I'll be in as soon as I feed my team."

From the way Dad spoke, the salesman thought there was no one in the house, so he walked into the kitchen without knocking. I was kneeling with my back to the door, putting clean paper on the lowest shelf of the cupboard. Assuming Dad had come in, I said, without looking up, "I made you an apple pie for dinner. You ought to love me for that."

A strange voice answered, "Indeed I shall."

We had quite a laugh.

Meanwhile the land acquisition was being completed. The bank sold the land of the Scotts and both Brewer families. The three places were on the same section of land, but one went for twenty-two dollars an acre, one for twenty dollars, and one for fifteen dollars. The bank sold the land to the government for exactly what it was mortgaged for. Each dispossessed family received one hundred dollars to move.

Woodger had disappeared from the scene. Dad signed an option with the new agent. He would get a little more than twenty-two dollars an acre and could stay until May, 1936. I didn't like it much, but Mama wanted him to sell. He could not afford a lawyer fee to go to court for more money, so that seemed the best deal he could get. At least he would be paid for his hay meadows, had a chance at another crop of hay and grain, and could dispose of his livestock and machinery in a leisurely way at the best price available in the next fifteen months.

February 12, 1935, Tuesday

Yesterday we had a thaw, and melting snow kept water in the low place under the swings. The youngsters spent the noon hour and recesses trying to scoop it out. After school Dora raced Carl for a swing, slipped, and landed in the puddle. Lona, looking gravely on, remarked, "Well, she either splashed out or soaked up all that water."

A man named Nelson, who is hired to administer federal relief in this county, has taken the unusual step, for a bureaucrat, of trying to find out what the score is. He came up in this neighborhood looking for Dad, and someone directed him to the schoolhouse to ask me where Dad was. He came just as school was dismissed and I was helping the children with their wraps.

As soon as they left, Mr. Nelson told me, "There is a girl going out the gate using most unladylike language."

"I gave her zero on her test because she was cheating. If you think her language is bad, stick around and get a real treat when her fond mama finds out I gave the kid zero."

Dirt was blowing into the schoolhouse until the air was just a haze. He asked if it would do that all spring.

"Probably. The northwest corner of Stutsman County has already blown in, but there are Foster and Wells Counties to come."

He looked thoughtful. "There are drawbacks to teaching in a place like this. You must have an interesting life, but do you like it? It seems to me you are wasting your life here."

I told him I like it all right and am used to it—my country, my home, my people—but mind the everlasting poverty because we could do so much here if only we had a little money. As it is, we just wait year after year for good times to come again.

Mama's sister in northern California has written urging me to come out and stay with her as she is sure I can get a job out there at better pay. It is tempting, but the way things are it seems better to stay closer to home.

March 14, 1935, Thursday

Last weekend Grover and I had a visit. We are both very concerned about the land. Dad's option hasn't been picked up. Nothing had been done about Grover's and Grandma's land, but the government is doubtless waiting until all the other land is sewed up, then our family, as the only holdouts, will have our land condemned. Losing her home would just kill Grandma. That is all Grover shows concern about, but I am also concerned, as I know he is, about what he will do and who will take care of Ted.

Grover is always cheerful, but has really had it rough. Dad was grown up, but Grover only three years old and his dearest pal, Uncle Herbert, only six, when they were left fatherless. Those little boys didn't have much of a childhood—there was too much work to do. They both graduated from the A.C., Herbert in mechanical engineering and Grover in farm husbandry. Grover came back to work his mother's place and acquire and develop his own ranch. Times were booming. Meanwhile Herbert enlisted in the Air Corps in the World War.

And what happened after the war? Farm prices dropped drastically, but not expenses. Grover had the responsibility of keeping the old homestead going and trying to develop Pelican Roost. Dad was married and had his own many acres and family to care for, their brothers Will and Herbert were dead, and Ted's health has steadily failed. It was up to Grover. Through years of backbreaking labor he has taken care of Grandma's ranch and his own, for which he is offered by the government less than he owes against it. There seems no way, now, he can save Grandma's place and Pelican Roost. What is he going to do? The stupidity and callousness of the land acquisition agents just appalls me. The kind of men Washington, D.C., sends out here destroys my faith in our government.

The schemes of Roosevelt and his Brain Trust to settle the country's problems are just costing money that in the long run will come out of the hides of the little people. When he got on the radio to talk to farmers, saying, "You are a fahmah, I am a fahmah," that rich man from Hyde Park was enough to turn a North Dakota farmer's stomach.

Bud has been ill with an appendicitis attack. His doctor bill put a hole in my last pay check. There is still $100.00 owed on Ethel's appendicitis operation because for the last two months I've had to buy feed for all the horses. I've kept only $7.00 from my pay since Christmas and am almost barefoot again—gotta buy some sturdy shoes.

March 20, 1935, Wednesday

This is the day before spring begins, and it is snowing to beat the band.

Friday afternoon the kids and I took a break from routine and made birdhouses for them to put up at their homes and then toasted marshmallows in the old jacket stove.

Saturday I rode to visit Grover, who was hauling hay. He got quite a kick out of my tale of woe about Dora. Her family is quarantined because her older brother has scarlet fever. Her mother told me she'd send Dora to school anyway. I said not without a doctor's permit because the other children must not be exposed. She insisted she would send Dora to school. It is useless to argue with her. Dora is so *much bigger than I am that if she got in the door, no way could I get her out. As she is too big to get in the window, I keep the door locked. The other children and I get in and out of the schoolhouse by crawling through the window.*

Monday evening about sunset I went out for a horseback ride. Dad called to me to drive in a heifer who was out of the pasture about half a mile north. I drove her back along the fence but was not tending to business because of gawking back at a red sunset and a flock of geese silhouetted against it. Somehow the heifer got up on the bank next to the fence. She couldn't get down, and I couldn't get up there.

Cliff, who was rounding up his horses in the flat, shouted to me, "What did that darn fool cow go up there for?"

"You'll have to ask her. It was entirely her idea. If it was up to you to get her down, how would you do it?"

"I woudn't. I'd tell her to stay there until Hell freezes over and come home on the ice."

Just then she jumped the fence into the pasture, and I rode on to enjoy the sunset.

In April of 1935 the dust storms temporarily ceased because there were several rains. The farmers, hopeful as ever, wanted to put in another crop. Only Dad and Grover could. The situation of the farmers on that future federal game refuge was puzzling. There had not been a crop for years. Each spring most of the farmers had mortgaged the crop they hoped to raise to buy feed, seed, and other supplies. Each year the crop had failed, leaving the farmer the mortgage to pay and no money to pay it, no feed and no seed, so he would take out another mortgage. With the exception of Dad and his brothers, everything those fellows had was mortgaged to the hilt. They dared not sell even an old and useless cow because she was mortgaged. In the spring of 1935 the government was making seed loans. The farmers at Stony Brook could not get them because they were on government land. They could not get off the government land because they had not been paid and had no money to go elsewhere. All they would get would be one hundred dollars apiece, but they hadn't even been able to collect that.

May 15, 1935, Wednesday
Last week I helped the kids make gifts for Mother's Day and had a struggle getting Leo to make anything.

Saturday night Cap and I went to the movie, Wallace Beery in Pancho Villa.

Sunday I was in the saddle all day, first helping Dad move his cattle and then Grover and Ted move theirs.

The weather has been so cold and drizzly not much spring work is done in the fields. Yesterday it warmed up. After school I did a big ironing and then raked and pitchforked the Russian thistle the wind has piled up at the bushes and garden fence. Milly Brewer came down, and we made a bonfire of the thistles. Then I walked partway home with her. These spring evenings are glorious—still and misty with sleepy birds calling. Peace and hopefulness lie over the Stony Brook country on evenings such as these.

By that time the government men were putting dams in the river and one in Stony Brook on land of Dad's they hadn't paid for. Arnold Friedman was furious about the deal he got. The Friedman house, some years previously, had cost nine thousand dollars, which would build quite a home in those days. All the government would give for the house, the other good buildings, and a quarter-section of land was fifty-six hundred dollars. The land acquisition agent promised the money in the fall, so Arnold sold the horses and machinery. The money still hadn't come. He had no equipment to put in a crop, no money with which to move—nothing.

Since I would get only one more paycheck, Dad was selling some of his livestock for money to keep things going on the place and to send Ethel to summer school. By thus making up for the quarter she quit mid-term at the Agricultural College in the spring of 1934, she could graduate from the teacher's college in the spring of 1936.

June 1, 1935, Saturday
I'm so pleased! Roany has always had a makeshift bridle I cobbled up out of an old one. When Dad sold some livestock he bought me a new

russet leather bridle for Roany, handmade and so handsome on that horse. Mama complained we had plenty of other places to put the money, but he said, "I'd have a hell of a time running this place without Ann and Roany. They deserve something."

School let out for the year last Wednesday. Thursday we went to Pingree for the Memorial Day program. That evening I was amused at Joe. He had the job of planting the acre of potatoes. He will not plant potatoes except at a certain phase of the moon which, this year, did not come until Memorial Day. Meanwhile I had planted enough in the vegetable garden to ensure that we have some to eat at the usual time. Dad likes to have new potatoes to eat when the green peas are ready.

Joe spent Memorial Day planting spuds in the field north of the garden. First he would plow a furrow, then leave his team while he dropped the cut potatoes the whole length of the row, then cover the potatoes with the dirt from the next furrow as he plowed it.

Once he left the team next to the garden while he dropped the potatoes. The garden looked good to King, who reached over the fence until he fell headlong over it. It took Joe twenty minutes to untangle the horses, fence, and harness. He cussed the whole twenty minutes without repeating himself once. Dad and I couldn't help him because the cattle we were to drive were already loose.

This weekend we had the end-of-school picnic at the lake and a good time. Almost everyone in the neighborhood came. One of the women was kind enough to tell me her grandson says he will miss school no. 3 and me, remarking to her, "All our other teachers had mouths that turned down all the time. Miss Ann is always laughing and joking and making things fun to do."

Bud came home from college today. It is so good to see him. We have been talking a blue streak.

That June it was dry again, and again we were plagued with dust storms. After each storm I had an all-day job cleaning everything in the house.

Grover, faced with the loss of his land, planned to go out and look over the Badlands in late June, during a slack period in farm work, and asked me to go along. I could get away, too, during that slack period because Bud would be home to help with the work.

During the time between spring quarter and summer school Ethel decided to go with some friends to a Chautauqua show in Wisconsin. Mama, doubtless still piqued about my new bridle, demanded that I give Ethel the $30.00 I was saving toward my insurance premium in the fall. That worried me. It had taken all spring to save $30.00 out of the $9.40 I kept from my check each month. In June I had no job in sight and did not want to risk letting the insurance lapse, but there was no need to worry. I got a job.

Grover and I left for the Badlands on Thursday, June 20, and spent twelve hours on the trip, with a stop at the museum in Bismarck. Of that trip I wrote:

Friday was a busy day in Medora because of the Stockmen's Convention. The hotel help was swamped with 80 to 90 dinners and suppers. I worked in the kitchen until 9:00 P.M., then dressed up and went to the dance, which was a lot of fun.

Saturday morning I applied for a job in Medora and also at a school north of town, though there are no vacancies at this time. In the afternoon Lee, Aunt Nettie, Grover, and I went north to Peaceful Valley.

Sunday we were invited to the branding at the Follis Ranch. It is owned by 80-year-old Bill Follis, who came up here in the Territorial days with the Texas trail herds. Lee, Uncle Fred, Grover, and I went. We had 43 miles of extremely bad roads, so got there too late for the branding, though the cattle were still there. The whole crowd had a good lunch out in the shelterhouse. Afterward some of the men played cards while the others took the cattle back to the range. We women did the dishes and visited.

Later in the afternoon Mr. Follis offered to show Grover and me Bullion Butte. It appeared the butte was only about a mile away, but the car registered seven miles when we reached the place from whence we had to hike another mile or so. We paused at "The Fountain of Youth" to drink the best spring water I ever tasted.

Then up and up to a big surprise. Completely hidden in a grove of trees were a barn, corral, and a stone and log house. Running water was piped into this vacant house from a spring. The lower floor was one great room with a huge fireplace at one end of it and a good floor for dancing. Later Lee told us the place had been the homestead of

Mr. Follis's daughter. Mr. Follis's second wife got it as part of the divorce settlement and lost it to the present owner, the Bank of North Dakota. The buildings are about halfway up Bullion Butte. The whole butte belonged to Mr. Follis once. Lee does not know but suspects, he says, the Bank of North Dakota owns it all now.

From the buildings we climbed to the top, which is level and spacious, with fine grazing land and a spectacular view of the buttes and canyons below. Zane Grey would love such a setting!

Tuesday I hiked and went driving with Laura. Then Uncle Fred wanted to show Grover and me the ranches for sale south of town. As we drove past the Knight place he said, "Ann, you want to live in the Badlands. I'll tell you how to manage it. Marry one of these eligible bachelor ranchers. Knight is a millionaire and spends all his summers here on his ranch. Or there is Hastings—a very handsome man."

"I think I prefer the Badlands' scenery without a husband mixed up in it. As for Knight—there are 150 pounds too much of him, and he is always drunk. As for Hastings—he's just a solid mass of conceit."

Uncle Fred laughed so hard he could scarcely drive. The ranch he especially wanted to show us was the Tutley spread, which did not appeal to Grover. That evening Johnny Taylor took us through his coal mine, which we found interesting.

Wednesday Uncle Fred, Grover, Laura, and I went all through the Badlands, to Beach, Golva, into Montana, to Marmarth, where we had lunch, and to Rhame, where there is a vacancy I applied for. The superintendent informed me a girl from Minneapolis, with a Master's degree and three years' experience, is also after the job. That is that. From there we went to Bowman and Belfield, then back to Medora and attended another dance that night.

Thursday we went about forty miles north to the Smith Ranch and watched the men brand 157 calves. The Smith Ranch must have been quite a spread in its day.

We left early Friday morning and got home between 5:00 and 6:00 P.M. Grover is not much impressed with the Badlands. He didn't like the range or the roads. I liked the Tutley spread next to the Custer Trail, but he thinks it would take too much money to swing either one. There was one thing neither of us liked: at both brandings two men, either bank or government agents, were sitting on the corral fence tallying the cattle. Everything must be mortgaged out there, too.

July 9, 1935, Tuesday
Cap and I went to the dance at the lake the night of the 4th. Vern was there. As he danced with me he said I am the only girl he ever loved and Marie, his wife, knows it. He says when he told her so, she threw her wedding ring in his face. I suggested he got a better wife than he deserves. I'd have thrown a hot flatiron in his face!

Friday I rode to the Big Pasture. The grass hasn't burned up yet this year, and the cattle are getting fat. Juneberries are ripening on bushes not killed by the drouth.

By that time a group of barracks were being built south of the lake for a CCC camp. The Civilian Conservation Corps had been established by the government to give young men work and train them for jobs. A $39,000 headquarters was being built at the southwest corner of Arrowwood Lake. CCCs cleared the ground.

In July there was a vacancy in the Cleveland, North Dakota, school. Dad took me there to apply. One board member wanted to hire me, but the president of the board, who controlled the third member, was politically against Dad and would not consider me.

Mama was not able to do much that summer because her varicose veins were bothering her. In July the doctor ordered her to bed for a month. Work was piling up for haying and harvest. I could not take care of Mama, do all the housework, tend the garden and poultry, and work in the fields, too, so Dad hired another man—Al. He was an aging widower, but not nearly as old as Joe and not crippled with rheumatism. The men managed the long hours of field work and care of the horses. Bud took over the milking and care of the milk, the calves and the hogs, checked the Big Pasture, and worked in the fields when he could.

August 7, 1935, Wednesday
Mama's legs are getting better due to staying strictly off her feet. I've been very busy. There is the cooking for Dad, Bud, two hired men, Mama, and me, a nine-room house to keep clean, the washing, ironing, baking, churning, tending a big garden, canning fruits and vegetables, and raising chickens and turkeys. Those turkeys keep me on the run, especially in the evenings. They don't have sense enough

to come home to roost, and I have to run all over 640 acres to get them in before the coyotes start hunting. It would be nice to keep them penned up, but they must rustle most of their feed because we can't afford to buy them any. They do help keep the grasshoppers down.

It took until midnight to finish canning peas last night. If I had known all those peas would grow, I wouldn't have planted so many. It would be impossible to manage except that dear Bud gives me a hand whenever he can. Tonight, when it was almost dark and not all the turkeys rounded up, he came striding through the fields to help me, singing, "I Want to Sing like the Birdies Sing—Cheep—Cheep—Cheep—Cheep—Cheep."

To add to all the other joys, we have civil engineers, surveyors, and CCCs underfoot all the time. The surveyors have spent enough time on this 640 acres to have it surveyed into ten-foot lots. The engineers keep coming around to ask dumb questions. The CCCs are not on our property, but stare as I ride by after the mail. One once called out asking to ride my horse with me. I told him to get a donkey—they would make a good pair. None of them has said anything to me since.

Just for example, this is what we had on this place last Monday: surveyors all over the east meadow, CCCs all along the north road, a CCC foreman of no announced purpose, two engineers looking for the foreman, a truck driver looking for chickens to buy, an engineer who thought this was the road to the lake, and a U.S. marshall with some papers about Dad's land they put a dam on last April. Oh, how I wish the government had stayed out of my Stony Brook country! It is all spoiled.

Milly Brewer's family, since rust got their crop and there was nothing to harvest, have already moved away to a small farm near Kensal. It is not much of a place, but all they could rent for the $100 they have a promise of when they move. I'm going to miss Milly.

Her uncle, George Brewer, is the only man who has gotten his money since the bank sold his place from under him. He was paid $200 above what his mortgage was bought for. The reason is there is a gravel pit on his place. The government wanted the gravel for work on the refuge. By paying him off now, they can use his gravel without paying him for it.

August 16, 1935, Friday

I've had a letter from the school board at Cleveland saying they had looked up my qualifications and decided to hire me. It was a satisfaction to write them I have another job. I've been hired at Courtenay, a town fourteen miles from home.

Life is becoming more hectic. Bud's appendix flared up again and he is in the hospital in Jamestown where the doctors will operate when the inflammation is brought under control. I teased him that he managed to get sick while Margaret was still at Trinity Hospital. She is about to graduate. Fortunately, most of the field work is done for the summer and Mama is now able to be on her feet some of the time.

Bud recovered fast from the operation and was able to go back to college as soon as it started. I had been able to finish paying for Ethel's operation of the year before with my last paychecks the previous spring. By the end of August Dad was worrying about Bud's doctor and hospital bill of two hundred dollars and the cost of continuing to keep Ethel and Bud in college. The crop, which had been promising that year, was scarcely worth harvesting because rust got into it. The cattle were doing well, but there was no price for them. The turkeys, which had also done well, would not be ready for market until November. What were we going to do?

Much as I loved Dad and sympathized with him, I was tired and cross, penniless and destitute for clothes. Mama, who sewed beautifully, could, at little expense, make me some dresses for the start of school in Courtenay, but not shoes and stockings. Come October, when the first paycheck was due, there would be that insurance premium to pay and the purchase of a winter coat, hat, gloves, overshoes, and various other things. I could give no help until November but thereafter could probably contribute fifty dollars a month again to pay Ethel's expenses and whittle down the other bills. My salary was seventy-five dollars a month, and board and room only twenty-one dollars. If Dad could scat up the money, even by borrowing, to get us all started in September, he could repay that debt with turkey money in November and have enough turkey money left to keep things going at home. With that, and the cream and egg money, we ought to be able to get by for another year.

Bud, after the initial cost of clothes, books and tuition, earned enough in spare time to cover his room and board and other things he needed. I don't recall whether Dad borrowed money to get us started or not, but somehow we managed.

By late August about twenty buildings were completed at the CCC camp just west of the eighty acres Dad owned up at the lake. A superintendent named Dowson was in charge of the boys during working hours. The rest of the time they were in the charge of army officers. It was to be a five-year camp with two hundred CCCs stationed there.

We didn't like having that camp in our neighborhood, and the camp personnel didn't like being there. They made no secret of the fact they considered us a bunch of yokels living in a mess of geology poorly begun and never finished. Furthermore, we were Republicans with no appreciation of the finer things the New Deal was going to do for us.

August 24, 1935, Saturday

The men moved into camp last Wednesday, one of them suffering from quinsy. The camp has an Army doctor, Dr. Anson. The only time I've seen that critter he was drunk down at the pavilion. Yesterday the sick boy got so bad the doctor told Dowson he would soon have to lance the boy's throat. Then he left on some errand he didn't explain.

The camp has hooked its telephone line (without consent or invitation) into our Stony Brook line. So we amuse ourselves listening to their telephone calls. Yesterday afternoon the men at camp were frantically phoning around trying to locate Dr. Anson. The boy was slowly choking to death because his throat had not been lanced. There is a doctor in Kensal, ten miles from camp. Carrington and Jamestown, respectively twenty and thirty miles from camp, each have several doctors and a hospital. Did they try to take the boy to any of these places? No, indeed, they must use the Army doctor.

About five o'clock Dr. Anson phoned camp to ask what they wanted.

"Nothing now. The patient died an hour ago."

The parents have no comeback. They sign papers when a boy enters CCC that they cannot be recompensed by the government if anything happens.

This morning I rushed out to ask Joe where Dad was, as there was a long-distance call for him.

"Vell-ll, ven I vas goin' to feed de calves, he came down by de turkey yard und told me not to feed de calves yet because dey vas vay up in de pasture, und it vould take too long to get dem down. Den I came back vit de milk und he vas valking to de garage—"

"Where is he now?"

"Oh, he's out in de barn."

Joe would make a good politician or bureaucrat, he can talk so long without saying anything.

Not long ago Bud went out to help milk one morning and found my pet kitten lying dead in the alleyway.

"What happened to Ann's cat?"

"Vell-ll, I vas lettin' de cows in, und Elizabet came in first, den de Holstein, den Lulu, den de roan, den Mary und Rosy. Und de Holstein vent in her place all right, but Lulu vent in de roan's place, und de roan knocked her avay, und she hooked de Holstein, und de Holstein she stepped back—"

About that time Bud got tired of it. "Do you mean a cow stepped on the cat?"

"Yais, dat's vat I said!"

I've read in the paper an article about what makes a successful rural school teacher.

"In calling attention to the requirements for a successful rural school teacher, someone has suggested that she must be primary, intermediate, grammar grade, and high school teacher combined; that she must be able to build fires, adjust fallen stovepipes, put in windowpanes, sweep, dust, split kindling, drive a car, keep out of neighborhood quarrels, know how and where to whip a bad boy, understand school laws, raise money for libraries, keep all kinds of records, plant trees on Arbor Day, be of good moral character, and pass an examination of the branches of modern education.

"For these accomplishments, she receives $40 to $50 a month. Out of this she pays room and board, buys her clothes, attends summer

school, buys educational books and papers, attends county con-
ventions, and furnishes pencils for her pupils. What is left she adds to
her bank account or starts a bank if she prefers."

The Courtenay school opened September 9. It was a well-
equipped school for a small town at that time. I boarded, with the
other unmarried teachers, at a home across the road from the
schoolhouse and roomed at a home in the northwest corner of
town. It was a dull little town, but I liked my work there as well as
the other teachers and the townspeople.

October 2, 1935, Wednesday
School is going well, and I enjoy life here, but there is nothing special to
write about. This is one of those innumerable little towns along the
Soo Railroad where nothing ever happens but morning, noon, and
night.

  Friday Cap took me home. We stopped in to see his stepmother,
who looks very thin and ill. She says she is feeling fine except for a
persistent cold.

  The CCCs are making a duck pond in the Big Pasture now. With
Caterpillar tractors and about 100 men they are changing the course
of the river a few feet in one place. There's nothing like improving on
Nature. While they were about it they cut the pasture wires. I worked
all day Sunday getting the cattle back in and fence fixed.

  The George Brewer family and the Scotts have moved away.

  Dad is busy plowing firebreaks. There has been no rain this fall. He
has not plowed firebreaks for many years, but is scared of the CCCs
with their careless use of matches and cigarettes.

October 20, 1935, Wednesday
Friday Cap came to take me to the dance in Edmunds. From there I
intended to go to Jamestown to stay with Audrey for the weekend and
take in the J.C. Homecoming. Those plans got changed. As I danced
with Arnold Friedman, he told me to go home as Dad would need my
help to move the cattle out of Section 6. I told Arnold he must be
mistaken—that is all the fall pasture Dad had, and he certainly would
not move his cattle out of it now.

Arnold said he was not mistaken, adding, "There have been people living on the newly made federal game refuge for more than fifty years, and none of them ever managed to burn it up. But the CCCs were so afraid some dumb farmer would start a prairie fire they just burned everything in sight so that couldn't happen. And if the farmers weren't so narrow-minded they'd give three cheers for the CCC boys instead of being mad—because think what a good idea it was—even if they did thousands of dollars worth of damage."

This is what happened: since everything is dry as tinder this fall, Dad and Grover, worried about CCC negligence, plowed firebreaks around their buildings.

Last Thursday the Camp Superintendent, Dowson, got the bright idea a firebreak was needed on the old Woods farm behind Grandma's place, where there has been no grazing since the government took it over. He told a foreman and a CCC boy to make one. Dowson was there, but apparently knew nothing of making a firebreak. The stupid foreman plowed just two furrows, a short distance apart, with the idea of forming a firebreak by burning between the furrows. Probably he read a book sometime, but he should have turned the page. Plowing just two little furrows with dry knee-high grass and weeds between them, and a high wind blowing, was pretty dumb. A blind man with his head down a well could see that would start a prairie fire.

The fire headed straight for Grandma's house, where she was sick in bed. Dowson sent the CCC boy back to camp to get all the men. He took his trousers off to beat out the fire. That ended his trousers; the fire roared on like Hell's delight.

Arnold saw the fire break out and got there as soon as the truckloads of boys did. He said it was comical to see them try to fight the fire, which would be burning yet if Dad hadn't come, organized the boys, and showed them how to fight it. They were just standing in front of it flapping wet gunnysacks at it. The men who were supposed to be in charge of them did nothing but stand around with mouths agape.

Dad had been seeding rye on his 80 acres at the lake close to the CCC camp. The government never picked up his option. Not planning to give them another or to move in May of 1936, he is putting in another crop. He saw smoke rolling over the hills and promptly started for home nearly two miles away.

Joe and Al were picking corn in the flat where they couldn't see the smoke. Al said, "I looked up all of a sudden and saw the boss headin' for home. I wouldn't 'a thought anything about it—s'posed he'd broke down—on'y I saw all four horses were on the run and the boss was hittin' Daisy to make her go faster. Now, when I saw the boss pourin' leather to Daisy, I sure as shootin' knew somethin' was wrong. So I shouts for Joe to come on, and we beat it for home right behind the boss."

Dad jumped in the car and rushed over to take charge of the firefighters. By that time the whole valley was full of smoke. Aunt Evalyn kept the trouble a secret from Grandma by pulling down her window shade and saying the smoke was due to a firebreak Ted was burning.

The fire raged over the hills and into the coulees, burning all the fall pasture Grover and Ted had. What saved Grandma's buildings was the firebreak Grover had plowed clear down to the river. No one lives on Aunt Em's property. Everything there burned but the windmill, and the shaft of that burned halfway up. Grover's calf barn burned to the ground. They never stopped the fire until it got to the flat, where plowing Ted had done checked it in spite of the high wind.

On Friday it started again. The first fire burned a strawstack of Ted's. The CCCs kept a guard there Thursday night, but didn't have sense enough to keep a guard until the stack stopped smoldering. Friday noon the wind scattered some burning straw into the grass, and there was another prairie fire. That burned all Dad's fall pasture and some hay.

By the time Dad got to that fire, he was mad. So was Dowson, who yelped, "Somebody must have set this fire."

"Somebody certainly did. Your men set it yesterday," and Dad showed him how it started again.

It took those 200 CCCs all afternoon to get it out. Grover says he didn't help fight that fire at all, but just drove the cattle to safety. As he rode home he passed a boy doggedly pounding away with a wet gunny sack and saying, "We were supposed to have the afternoon off."

Well, after the dance I didn't go to the J.C. Homecoming, but spent the weekend helping with the cattle. Grandma is getting better and still knows nothing of the fire.

November 6, 1935, Wednesday

Dad came after me Friday to help work cattle. He says now that the calf barn is burned and snow has come, Grover will have to sell his calves at a loss. Dowson refuses to try to get any settlement for the barn and declares that if Grover sues for damages, he and all his men will swear that the fire was "an act of God." He also refuses to do anything about the lost pasture. There is a lot of pasture land on the refuge that has not been touched by fire or grazing this year. He could just as well let Dad and Grover use at least as much as he burned.

Dad says Dowson has set himself up in his own mind as a dictator like Hitler, and he knows his mind pretty well.

I reckon his mind is not a place he'd care to be cooped up in very long. The Stony Brook country used to have decent, hard-working inhabitants. They had their faults, like everyone else, and some were narrow-minded on religious matters, but they were good-hearted and helpful to one another. I have never had occasion to meet the kind of lallygagging sidewinders the government is sending here, and I don't like them. I want to get out of here.

Saturday I worked at home and went to visit Grandma, who is much better. That evening Cap came to tell me his stepmother has T.B. and has been given six months to live. We feel awful about it. Her married daughter in town will take care of her until she can be sent to the T.B. sanitarium in the northern part of the state.

November 12, 1935, Tuesday

Mama writes the CCCs have torn down every building on the Brewer and Scott places. She also says, "Joe has invented a contraption for shelling corn for the turkeys. Edison with his incandescent light could have been no prouder. It is the end of an apple box with two sections of mower sickle. He puts the board on a kitchen chair, sits on it, and draws corn cobs between the two knives. He shelled corn all over the kitchen last night. I even found a kernel in the teakettle this morning."

Cap writes his stepmother has made out a bill of sale turning all the livestock over to him, and he is to look out for his two youngest half-sisters and get them through high school. Imagine a bachelor with two teen-age girls to raise! It is enough to make me wish I could marry him and help. But I have my own folks to think of, and sometimes it seems I have enough to do.

Bud wrote thanking me for an extra $5 I sent him. He can't spend the money to come home for Thanksgiving, but will have nearly three weeks at Christmas.

In spite of stormy weather and bad roads, Dad took me home for Thanksgiving. He said the superintendent and officers at the CCC camp were pestering him to bring in a county snowplow to clear the half-mile of road between camp and the county road. Stutsman County, a very big county, had only two snowplows. Dad couldn't call one in to plow out the camp. Farmers, with their ancient cars, were getting along fine in the snow. CCCs, with all their manpower and expensive new trucks, tractors, and pickups, could not seem to manage. They failed to plan ahead and had to make frequent trips to town for supplies.

Christmas vacation was the next visit home.

December 24, 1935, Tuesday
This is the strangest Christmas Eve I've ever spent!

This morning Mama and Dad and Bud went to Jamestown to do some shopping. I planned to ride to Grandma's with the Christmas presents, just as I've done the day before Christmas since I was eight or ten years old. It was a fine sunny morning.

By the time the housework was done and I could start, it was 12:30 and clouding up. I dressed warmly and was not alarmed that it was getting colder. Just as I reached the dam a furious blizzard struck— faster than I've ever seen a storm hit. There was no time to get to shelter, the temperature was plummeting rapidly toward 30° below, the snow was so thick I couldn't see a thing and couldn't tell direction because the wind kept changing direction. I told Roany to go home. Soon I realized my face was freezing and dismounted to thaw it out, nearly freezing my hands in the process. Ice had coated over Roany's eyes until he was blinded.

Getting home was a nightmare of cold and stinging snow. I had to keep getting off Roany to break the ice away from his eyes, but was getting very stiff and numb. I thought of hanging onto the stirrup and walking, but could not walk far in the deep snow. Since it was impossible for either of us to see anything but swirling snow, I could not tell if Roany was going home or simply drifting with the wind. At last he stopped—right in front of the barn door.

I thankfully rolled off, turned the horse over to Joe, and went to the house to thaw out. My face, hands, and feet are frostbitten, but not badly. The storm is still going strong tonight. I helped Al and Joe string a clothesline from the house to the barn so they wouldn't get lost going back and forth to do chores. They are now sitting here playing cards and eating fudge. We haven't heard from the folks, but are not worried. Dad would never start home in such a storm. We hear the telephone lines are down in the Jamestown area, so he can't call us.

Our telephone line isn't down. Except for the time it took to cook supper and do dishes, I've spent this stormy afternoon and evening listening in on the CCC camp. They have very little coal. Captain Meyers was supposed to have ordered it, but he didn't. He went to Kansas City ten days ago and isn't due back until sometime in January. Dowson is snowbound in town and Dr. Anson snowbound in camp. Anson is really making the phone tingle over that sad fact. The trucks went to town for coal and can't get back. The CCCs, of whom only about 90 are in camp over Christmas, are crowded into one building and are burning furniture to try to keep warm. They are constantly telephoning their plight to Dowson. He really can't do anything about it and obviously doesn't care.

Our furnace is acting up. The wind is so strong it sucks the fire right up the chimney. I'm keeping the fire very low for fear of setting the house on fire, so it's chilly in here. Ethel went to bed to keep warm. I am going to stay up all night to keep the furnace fired, but not too much. The men offered to spell me at tending furnace. I won't hear of it. They have had a hard day tending livestock and are apt to have a hard one tomorrow. They need their sleep.

December 30, 1935, Monday

The storm continued all night the night before Christmas, and I stayed up all night tending the furnace. Christmas morning dawned clear, sunny, and 28° below zero. After the chores were done, Al and I drove in the bobsled over to Grandma's with the Christmas presents. She *was surely glad to see us. Only Grover and Ted are with her for the holidays. Aunt Evalyn is in the hospital in Rochester, Minnesota, and Helen and Em are with her.*

After Al and I got home, Dad phoned from Kensal that he and Bud would walk home from there. The folks got through shopping fairly early on the 24th and were on the way home when that sudden storm struck. Bud tried to keep the Ford on the road and get home. They passed a lot of cars in the ditch and a schoolhouse where twenty people were stranded. When they got to Nevas' corner, ten miles from home, they could go no further. Fortunately, Nevas' house is near the road, and they could make it to the house on foot with no harm except Mama got frostbitten ears.

Nine other people were also marooned there, and Nevas have no telephone. Most of the people had groceries they had bought in Jamestown and took in to help Mrs. Neva feed the crowd. There was room for the women to go to bed. The men stayed up all night playing cards. Christmas day Kringlie took Mama and Dad and Bud to Kensal. Dad and Bud walked the seven miles home. Then Dad took the bobsled to town for Mama. There will be no getting the car home until a snowplow reaches this part of the county.

I must tell about the CCCs. Christmas morning Lt. Dunham called Dowson to say he'd sent three Caterpillars out to break the road to Kensal to liberate the trucks already there and was sending all the trucks still in camp behind the Cats. He told Dowson to have the trucks loaded with coal and sent back immediately. Dowson said he wouldn't. They had a government contract with Zimmerman in Edmunds, and the coal must be hauled from there. It wouldn't do to repeat what Dunham said, but the idea was they would freeze to death long before the Cats could get through the hills and over to Edmunds. Dowson was to send the coal from Kensal, or he, Dunham, would make him wish he had. They have hauled coal all day long every day since.

The storm was quite general over the state. A number of people caught in it froze to death.

Aunt Nettie writes she thinks there will be a vacancy at Sentinel Butte next year and a personal application might get me the job. She wants me to come out at Easter vacation and apply.

Windswept

This morning, at 5:45, I heard the snowplow coming, so got up and fixed a breakfast of mush, pancakes, and steak for the crew. The night crew slept here while the day crew took the plow on towards Edmunds.

CHAPTER 9

The Tempest

As 1936 arrived, I seemed to have great hopes for it.

January 3, 1936, Friday
Bud had to leave for college New Year's Day, so I got his clothes ready. I had given him money to buy a new winter coat and like his choice so well I gave him $3.00 to buy a hat to go with it. The kid is getting by, but has a hard time making enough for room and board without trying to squeeze out any money for clothes.

After he left, I went for a ride on Roany and thought hopeful thoughts for the new year. The last six years have been tough, what with the Big Depression, my inability to get a good paying job, illnesses, a thousand petty discouragements, crop failures, drouth, dust storms, poor cattle market, and now this game refuge thing costing us our home and Dad's work of a lifetime. Somehow we've made it so far. Surely in 1936 things will break for the better.

February 13, 1936, Thursday
This is the worst winter I ever saw. There is one blizzard after another, and for six weeks the warmest day has been 10 below zero. From there it has ranged down to 40 below. A number of days we have not held school because the buses can't travel.

I hear the CCC camp is having an awful time getting food and fuel. In this country people stock up on such things in the fall, but not these government geniuses. A couple of boys have died. The camp doctor could not or would not care for them and could not or would not send them to a nearby hospital. In spite of weather and road conditions, he tried to send them to Ft. Lincoln, 150 miles away. They didn't get there alive.

Cap, snowed in alone on the farm, writes regularly. His half-brother and two half-sisters still in school are staying with their married sister in town in order to get to school at all. He says the drifts in the yard are 18 feet deep, so he can't get a horse out, but occasionally walks to town on top of the drifts. He says he will never spend another winter like this and wants me to marry him when school is out. Yeah? The Stony Brook country I loved is gone forever with this game refuge thing and I am leaving—don't know how or where, but I'm getting out.

Last Friday a three-day blizzard started, and the weekend was a holy terror for cold and snow. Everyone who could stayed in bed to keep warm. My landlady came upstairs Sunday morning and found her little boy and dog and cat all in bed with me.

The president of the school board tells me I'll be re-elected next year, saying they are pleased that the kids like me and I also have good discipline. But how about more money?

February 19, 1936, Wednesday
Dad used to take the Fargo daily newspaper years ago before we were so hard up for money. Recently I got him a subscription. When he wrote to thank me he said they have been very busy trying to keep the livestock comfortable.

"The Strawberry Roan gets out for a few minutes before sundown every day. He bounces around some, stands on his hind legs, claws the cold air with his front feet, does some fancy bucking and quite a lot of equine acrobatics and then is glad to get back in his warm stall.

"They are having quite a bit of trouble at the camp during this spell of weather. Every time the wind blows they are out of coal. Since last Sunday they have smashed up two tractors and six trucks trying to get fuel to camp."

The snowbanks right on main street here are so high we can look into second-story windows as we walk down the street. We have not been able to hold school this week, but plan to tomorrow.

March 20, 1936, Friday

I'm away behind with this diary. The 8th of March I got a card from Mama saying Dad had walked over to Grandma's and she was just fine. She hadn't seen any of her relatives but Grover and Ted since Christmas. Everyone has been snowed in. Aunt Evalyn, after her operation in Rochester, in December, went to Tulsa to recuperate at Aunt Helen's house.

The week of the 8th the snow started melting. That Friday night Mama phoned me to come home and help. I was to take the train to Kensal Saturday morning, where Al would meet me with horses. Grover had come over to say Grandma had taken sick that day. He used our phone to call Aunt Em to try to get out to the farm. The CCC camp and our place have the only phones for miles around these days.

Saturday it was thawing. Al and I rode home from Kensal over roads that were lakes between huge snowbanks.

In the afternoon I rode to Grandma's. Was that trail a mess! Roany had all he could do to travel it. Aunt Em, looking worn out, reported the doctor had been there twice. She thought Grandma was getting worse. Dad would have to arrange to get Mama over there to help. I beat it home and helped Mama cook up a lot of food. Then Dad used a team of horses to get her and the food to Grandma's.

Sunday I baked meat, bread, cake, cookies, pie, churned, and fixed a stock of cottage cheese to help the men batch it that week. Dad took me back to Courtenay by car that evening. As far as number 9 it was a perilous trip. We would not have made it if three trucks and 58 CCCs had not happened to be ahead if us and making a trail we followed. I'll never forget that fourteen-mile ride over slushy roads and between towering snowbanks. It was a beautiful moonlight night.

The next Tuesday I got a letter from Unk, husband of Dad's sister Lydia. "Your mother asked me to drop you a line tonight. I have just returned from your Grandmother's. You of course know she is not very well. The doctor has found that her condition is much worse due to the heart which is not functioning as it should. He thinks it is just a matter of time until the end. Everything is being done that can possibly be done for her."

I called home and got Al, who said Grandma was very low and Dad and Mama both over there. I was just sunk at the idea of life without Grandma. I hadn't seen her since Christmas due to this terrible weather, and now might never see her again. It had been a dreary winter for her, snowbound in that isolated house. It seemed unbearable that she should die just when her loved and longed-for spring was coming. I don't ever waste time bawling, but couldn't help it that night. I just cried and cried.

Thursday Unk sent a card saying she was a bit better. That Thursday night Bud phoned me. He was home between quarters until the next Tuesday. Since things were in an upheaval at home, Ethel had decided to visit friends during spring break. Bud said Mama had been gone all week and he had been washing dishes all day. He wanted me home and would pick me up the minute school was out Friday. He did, too. It was so good to see him! We chattered a mile a minute all the way home.

The kid got no vacation at all—just work. He was such a good sport about it as he went around humming "Without a Song This Day Would Never End." We worked eighteen hours a day with chores, cooking, washing, ironing, baking, churning, etc. for both places and always running back and forth the 2½ miles with laundry and food, or taking messages because there is no phone at Grandma's place. Bud was right beside me, ready to turn a hand to anything whether he knew how or not, and humming "Without a Song."

As he took me home that Friday, I noticed the snow was going off slowly so the water can sink into the ground instead of causing floods. We can be thankful for that. At home were four hungry men to feed, and even the bread and butter were used up. I scatted up some supper, did dishes, then Bud and I hiked across country to Grandma's.

She was asleep. Aunt Evalyn was in bed, too, worn out by the trip she and Aunt Helen took from Tulsa, Oklahoma. We visited with Mama, Aunt Nettie, Aunt Helen, and Lee. The doctor had told Dad Tuesday night there was no hope for Grandma. Dad rushed home and phoned the Fergusons at Medora. Six hours later Lee and Aunt Nettie got as far as Jamestown. Dad also phoned Aunt Helen. She and Evalyn flew from Tulsa to Jamestown. Meanwhile Grandma had rallied. The doctor forbade them to see her because their presence at that time would indicate to her she was not expected to live.

That Saturday I did the washing and baking for both houses as Mama and the aunts were exhausted and had enough to do with the housework, getting meals, and looking after Grandma.

Bud churned the butter for both houses. I told him how much salt to put in it. He claimed it was too sweet and put in another handful. Then I tasted it and discovered he was using sugar instead of salt.

That afternoon, while I was ironing, Lee walked in, having gotten his car stuck in mud more than a mile away. Grandma was very low. He phoned Unk to try to get Aunt Lydia out there.

Bud went back with him to help get the car unstuck. I got supper and waited around, not daring to leave the house because someone had to be there in case of phone calls. Soon Dad and the doctor came. Dad was feeling terrible. His adored mother was dying. Aunt Helen had suggested, since part of the trouble was heart trouble, that he call in the heart specialist from Jamestown. The specialist could get to Pingree, and one of the men could meet him there and get him over the west road to Grandma's. Dad and the local doctor talked to the specialist, ate supper, and went back to Grandma. It had turned very cold and windy. I spent a long, dread-filled evening listening to the wind and waiting for word.

About 11:00 Dad and Bud walked home. Both doctors had been with Grandma all evening. The specialist changed the treatment and thought she was in no immediate danger.

Believing she was dying, the local doctor had permitted Helen and Evalyn to visit her for a few minutes because it would be too bad for them to get no chance to do so. Evalyn claimed she had intended to come home in March, but Grandma wasn't fooled and fussed about her sickness upsetting everyone's plans. She keenly resented the presence of both doctors, thinking them plumb unnecessary.

Sunday morning Dad, Bud, and I went back to Grandma's, where I visited with her briefly because she had been asking to see me. Mama was asleep. Evalyn is very thin and weak. I helped her with the dishes before coming home to do the work here. She told me Mama is quite tired and is worrying about getting Bud's clothes ready to go back to school and how the work will be done at home when I go back to Courtenay. I said to tell her not to worry. I'd tend to Bud's clothes and hire a substitute in order to stay home this week. The school board *will not hire substitute teachers but will permit us to hire anyone qualified and pay the substitute from our own pockets. The principal's wife agreed, by phone, to substitute for me.*

Monday I got up at 3:30 in the morning to get the washing and cooking done so Dad could go to Grandma's early. She had seemed better when he and I went over Sunday evening to get the laundry. Monday morning she was very sick due to another heart attack. In the afternoon Bud and I went over, taking more food. Helen and Lee had been to Jamestown to consult the heart specialist and brought home a registered nurse.

Tuesday Grandma was a little better. Bud took the 2:45 train from Kensal back to Fargo. Later Dad and I went back to Grandma's to get Mama. With the nurse there, she could be spared to come home and rest a few days.

Wednesday morning Grandma was weaker. Lee came to phone for both doctors again. Later the local doctor phoned me to say she was out of danger—they were sure she would live. Oh, what a relief after the terrible strain!

Yesterday and today I've worked at Grandma's half the day and at home the other half. The continued thawing has made the trail down Stony Brook impassible. I have to ride clear to the bridge south of Arrowwood Lake, follow a CCC road through Section 36, our former Big pasture, then strike across the tops of the hills back of Grandma's place to get there at all.

In Section 36 is a big pile of rubbish and tin cans lying out in the flat, one of many such piles scattered around the refuge. Yesterday Roany, surprised at the change of scenery, refused to go past it. While I was arguing with him, Dowson, whom I hadn't seen all winter, came along in a pickup. I'd have ignored him if he hadn't stopped.

"Does the refuge pass inspection this morning?" he asked in his sarcastic way.

"It is a refuge? That's what I've heard, but it looks like a garbage dump."

He drove away sputtering.

Grandma is better today. I visited with her—briefly, of course— then Helen and I had a good visit and much fun.

One of my pupils wrote to say she is sorry Grandma is sick. "Mrs.

Andrews is teaching us now. I like her. But I like you better. I miss you because you have so many jokes to tell and little stories that go along with the subjects. But we are getting along fine."

March 26, 1936, Thursday

All weekend, Mama kept me entertained with the stories of what had been going on at camp last winter. Her winter's amusement had been listening in on the phone conversations of the CCC camp.

I've previously mentioned what a time they had getting fuel at Christmas time. The captain and lieutenant were transferred in January, and a Captian Unger and Lt. Vettle sent here. Neither one can get along with Dowson.

A company clerk named Ellson usually answers the phone, in a perpetually disgusted voice. One can tell he is always just fed up with the whole outfit.

Unger and Vettle had 200 men in that camp ten miles from town, and with the roads blocked since Christmas. They were always trying to get food and fuel and always smashing up their equipment.

About the first week in February the snowplow got to Kensal and was, of course, under Dad's orders. Much as Dad detests the guys who run the camp, he has tried to help them out. He feels sorry for the 200 boys under them. Therefore, when he learned the plow was finally coming to his district, he asked Dowson if it would be better to have the plow go to camp first or Kensal first. Dowson said they could get from camp to #9, so it would be be best if #9 was cleared to Kensal first.

Dad sent the plow to town and then west of town to plow out the farmers there.

Next thing Mama heard Unger calling Dowson, who lives in town, to say the plow hadn't been seen at camp yet. Dowson didn't say he had asked Dad to send it to town first, but just said it was clearing a road west of town. Unger complained it was more important to clear a road for 200 men than for a few farmers. Dowson muttered that seemed to be a matter of opinion.

Then Unger phoned Dad that there was no need to plow the farmers out, and the plow should have been sent directly to camp when it got to this area.

Dad didn't tell him how two-faced Dowson was being, but told him the farmers did need to be plowed out. After all, the farmers were taxpayers who had paid for the road and plow and were entitled to some use of them. He had ordered the plow to camp when it finished the farm road. If Unger was not satisfied with that, and was in such a big hurry, well, the taxpayers were supporting him and all his men and had paid for all their equipment, including a lot of shovels not being used. They could just go shovel the road. Unger sputtered, but waited for the plow.

Not long after that the road to Edmunds, where the coal contract is, was temporarily open. Dad informed Dowson a storm was coming, so he better tell the Army officers to get coal that very evening. Dowson did. The Army officers, this being Friday and no one expected to do any work until Monday, did nothing about it.

The next day, Saturday, was a furious blizzard. Dowson could not get out of town. Neither could the snowplow. Vettle phoned Dowson to say it was so cold the coal was nearly gone.

"Why didn't you get some last night, as I told you?"

"Just didn't."

Sunday the weather let up a bit and Dowson got to camp. While he was there, Vettle and a driver went to Kensal in a pickup, followed by six trucks to haul coal. They made it to town, but it started blowing so hard they thought they couldn't get back. Meanwhile the snowplow had gone south to where #9 intersects the county road north of here which runs past the camp.

In the late afternoon Vettle called Ellson and said Dowson had just come back to town and told them for heaven's sake to take that coal to camp. Vettle wondered if they should or not.

"Dowson just drove in, didn't he?"

"Yes."

"Then he ought to know better than we do what the road is like."

"You think we should start out, then?"

"I think it would be the thing to do."

Vettle, in his pickup, was carrying gas for the snowplow, which did not have enough to get to camp. For no apparent reason, Vettle did not leave town until half an hour after the trucks did. By the time he left it was getting dark and the storm was rising again.

The snowplow had gone in the ditch near Forest's house. The crew was forced to take refuge at Forest's, where there is no phone, Vettle and his driver went in the ditch near the snowplow and were frozen about the face and hands before they got to safety at Forest's house.

Meanwhile the six trucks arrived at camp and Ellson was phoning around trying to locate Vettle. When informed Vettle left town half an hour after the trucks did, Ellson merely said, with bitter emphasis, "The damn fool!"

The camp spent the night phoning and sending search parties. By Monday there was such a fierce blizzard nothing could be done. Tuesday the storm let up, but it was frightfully cold. Vettle and the snowplow crew borrowed a team of horses from Forest to drive to town. The horses could not get through the drifts, which snapshots show to have been piled almost to the tops of telephone poles. However, the drifts were packed hard enough for the men to get on top of them and walk to town.

While they were walking to town, a search party found their pickup and, for some unexplained reason, took the snowplow's gas back to camp. So the snowplow was stalled with no way to get to camp where the gas was.

That snowplow was tied up for two weeks. Every time the crew tried to clear the road, another blizzard came up. The men in camp were burning everything in sight, including the old farm buildings. Once, in desperation, Dowson let them take the Army equipment to try to get coal. They smashed up six trucks and two Caterpillar tractors. Dowson would not authorize repairs out of Biological Survey funds. The Army would not pay because the Army officers had not authorized use of the equipment.

Unger, despairing of getting out of camp to his wife in town, phoned the State Highway Department. They told him every road in the state of North Dakota was blocked, and they certainly could not send a state plow to his camp. He would have to ask his county commissioner to send one.

Unger said he had done so, and the plow had not come.

"Your commissioner is doubtless doing the best he can, but he can't make it stop snowing. You will just have to count on him."

Unger has been quite courteous to Dad since then.

Zimmerman at Edmunds has the coal contract, but the road was seldom open in that direction. Once during the winter he phoned that the plow had come through and the camp could get coal from him.

"How much do you have?" Ellson asked.

"A ton and a half."

The camp was burning eleven tons a day.

Last Sunday I came back to Courtenay and school has gone on as usual.

Cap wrote, "Instead of sitting around here feeling so darned blue and lonesome, I will write a few lines to the dearest girl I know. You said we are drifting apart. But I'm going to make you care for me. We'll be married in the fall."

Phooey! Oh, I am fond of Cap, who is a very fine man, but I don't love him or intend to marry him. I'm just completely fed up with the way things are going in the Stony Brook country and am going to get out.

April 1, 1936, Wednesday
This week I'm busy as two pups with a feather duster. There is extra work with Girl Scouts, debating teams, and a declamation contest.

Lee wrote there is a vacancy at Sentinel Butte and gave me the names of the superintendent and school district clerk. "They are the ones to write to. Be sure and emphasize debating and declamation work you have done and also that you coach plays. The wages up there are $85.00. Medora wages are higher, but I don't think there will be any vacancies. Be sure and come out here at Easter, as I think it would be a good thing to see the Superintendent in person and let him see your personality. If you come out I will take you on a party and promise to show you a good time."

I have a job here for next year but want the Badlands if possible.

April 7, 1936, Tuesday
It is still cold for this time of year. I went home Friday and worked both there and at Grandma's Saturday. Grandma is getting along fine. I gave Aunt Helen the money to get her back to Tulsa. The expenses of Grandma's illness have taken every penny everybody in the family could possibly scrape up.

Good Friday was the tenth of April. The evening of the ninth I caught a ride to Jamestown with a fellow teacher and spent the evening with my old friend Audrey. The midnight bus, badly crowded, didn't arrive in Jamestown until 1:40 A.M. or in Medora until 9:00 A.M. That evening Lee took me to a party at the lodge at Painted Canyon, and Saturday afternoon took me to Sentinel Butte, seventeen miles west of Medora. There I put in personal applications to the superintendent and each school board member. The bus took all day Sunday to get back to Jamestown, where I stayed overnight with Audrey and caught a ride back to Courtenay.

Dowson, the camp superintendent, had been acting refuge manager at Arrowwood Refuge since 1934. When Grandma was sick in March, Grover told me the permanent refuge manager had come, a Harvard graduate from Boston in his first job with the government. Grover fairly wept with glee at the idea of a man from Boston managing the Arrowwood Refuge and coping with Dowson, Unger, Vettle, and the CCCs.

Later I asked Dad if he had met the manager and what he thought of him.

Dad said, "I think if anyone else on that game refuge had half the brains, ability, and common sense Seth Low has, they might have a game refuge someday."

As usual on Saturdays, I rode to see Grandma the last Saturday of April. Aunt Helen was gone, and a licensed practical nurse was staying with her. When I got home, the new refuge manager, Seth Low, was there talking to Dad. He stayed and talked to me while I did all the dishes piled up in the kitchen.

A week later I was riding through Section 36 on my way to Grandma's when Seth, up at headquarters a mile away, spotted me and arranged a "coincidence." Earl, the horticulturist at the CCC camp, came along in a pickup and asked me to see the plantings the CCCs had done in Section 36 under his direction. I left Roany grazing in the flat and went with him. Then we went to see the aquatic cellar. Next he suggested that we go to see headquarters. Seth was there using the living room as an office. He showed me the house, a six-room, one-story cinder block building, unfurnished, and much more suitable to the Florida climate than to that of North Dakota.

Earl took me back to Roany and I went to Grandma's. She was feeling fine.

May 14, 1936

Last week I got a letter from Seth saying "I should like to presume on our short acquaintance to the extent of asking if I might have the privilege of escorting you to the dance in Kensal this Friday evening."

Cap, though he knew I wanted to go to that dance, had not asked me. He could be sure no one else would because it was known I dated him. So I wrote Seth accepting the invitation but saying I could not leave Courtenay until after the operetta the school was putting on Friday night. I invited him to the operetta.

He wrote back that he had no car and Roy, a foremen at camp, had offered to take us to the dance. Friday evening they came in time to see the operetta before we went to Kensal.

Seth and I sat out in the car and talked quite a while. He said since he came here in February he kept hearing about me. The men at camp wondered why my family is the only one still on the refuge. Of course, Seth knows it is because Dad's, Grover's, and Grandma's land has never been purchased. He heard I am a teacher in Courtenay, reported to be very pretty, ride horseback a great deal, and will have nothing to do with anyone at camp. Some men said I am Dad's daughter; others, because I am with Grover so much, said I am his daughter. I laughed and laughed to hear all that gossip.

Then I found out a bit about him. He has always been interested in birds and has become quite an authority on them. He is the oldest of three sons, the other two working in the family business. Seth is not interested in that and, after graduating from Harvard in biology, worked at a research station on Cape Cod. There he could see no future. In 1935 he took an examination for a game refuge manager's job, hoping to get a position in Maine. Finally, in January, 1936, he was told he had passed the examination and would be manager of Arrowwood Waterfowl Refuge at Kensal, North Dakota, and was to report to the Regional Office of the Biological Survey in Minot, North Dakota, on February 1. No one he could contact had ever heard of

Kensal or the refuge. He could not find them on the map. However, he was on a train within twenty-four hours.

At Minot, about 170 miles from Kensal, he was given a government car and told to go to Arrowwood. The roads were temporarily open. In another day they were blocked again and the weather got very interesting.

Due to bad weather, no communications, no cooperation, and Dowson, who is almost insanely jealous over losing some of his authority, Seth has had a rough time of it. One day he saw me riding Roany and realized I am the girl named Ann he had heard about. He thought I looked attractive and tried to meet me, with no success. Then he met Dad and started spending time with Dad, partly for advice and partly in hope of meeting me. That is why he happened to be at our place one day when I rode home from Grandma's.

Finally we quit talking and went in to the dance. Cap was there and glared at me when I came in with Seth. I glared back and refused to dance with him. He was alone, but what was he doing there without me? He knew I wanted to go. He knew no local man would ask me when it was known I had been dating him for three years.

While we ate supper, Seth asked me about my boy friend. I told him what had happened and said Cap and I had probably just come to the parting of the ways. Then Seth said he wanted to be my boy friend. He wanted to have someone to take to dances and movies and had met no one except me with whom he had anything in common. I told him we could date for the summer; I am planning to leave in the fall.

May 20, 1936, Wednesday
Seth came down late Saturday afternoon, ostensibly to see Dad, but really wanting to talk to me. The men didn't get in for supper until 8:30. I asked Seth to stay because he had missed supper at camp, where they eat at 4:30. It was comical to hear him tell about the tree plantings. The government gave the refuge 40,000 young trees to plant. At that time there was moisture enough to plant them. Since then there has been no rain, and the ground is dried out. Now that they have gone through all the red tape, and gotten everyone to agree as to where the trees should go, it is too late to plant them. 40,000 trees wasted! Never mind, the taxpayers can pay for them.

It is so hot and windy the crops are blowing out again. Sunday I herded cattle, fixed fence, and came back to Courtenay.

School closed at Courtenay the end of May. Ethel, whose classes at the normal school had ended, was visiting a classmate. Bud was home from college and had a job as timekeeper for an oil-mix crew on Highway 7 near Carrington. For transportation he was buying a second-hand Model A Ford for seventy-five dollars. His job would pay for the car, and, he hoped, all of one semester's college expenses. Dad and Al and I would just have to manage without him. There had been no rain since April, so it appeared there would be little hay or grain to put up.

Poor old Joe, still trying but increasingly useless, helped with the barnyard chores. He was not worth what he cost us in board, clothing, and tobacco money. Now a man like him would have social security or some pension system. Joe had nothing. Our place was home to him, and it was up to people like us to take care of him.

The Big Pasture, state school land Dad had leased since 1900, had gone to the federal government for the refuge. Dad was left with the section we lived on and eighty acres at the lake. To replace the Big Pasture he rented land south of us. It was not as good pasture, but much closer to home and available for rent because the owner had lost it to the mortgagee.

A six-month option Dad had signed in the winter of 1935 permitted him to stay until May, 1936. The government never picked up the option, so he had seeded again and was keeping what livestock he could. Bud had a job for the summer. I hoped for one in the Badlands, but, if I didn't get it, was sure of one at Courtenay. Ethel was through school and might get a job. We would manage.

June 8, 1936, Monday
Thursday was hot and windy. Roy dropped Seth off here just as I was fixing supper. He stayed for supper. I laughed to hear him tell about how Roy teases him. Roy says, "It's just like a Zane Grey novel. Supply your own title. Eastern boy comes West—meets Western ranch girl—Eastern girl gets the go-bye—he falls for the cowgirl."

"There is even a villain," I said, "taking the old homestead."

Seth doesn't like it here and is discouraged. Dowson is hateful and fights him at every turn. Bell, who is director of refuges in this area, pays almost no attention to this refuge and blames Seth for things that happened before Seth ever came here. If this continues, he wants a transfer. Earl, the CCC horticulturist, has been fired. At the time he had 10,000 seedlings to be planted and was the only person who knew what they were. He dumped them, unlabeled, into the aquatic cellar. "Now let Dowson figure them out."

Seth wanted to go home early to do some work, but Roy didn't come after him when expected. I told him we have two railroad systems, out here—SE&W or CH&R—start early and walk, or catch a horse and ride. I lent him Roany to ride home. He used to spend his summers on a dude ranch in Wyoming and knows how to ride.

Friday afternoon Seth and a CCC civil engineer named Archie came and asked me to go with them to get my horse. Roany was refusing to eat or drink or allow anyone to come near him. He was getting downright bad-tempered.

They helped me with the dishes and ate pie until the bread was out of the oven and I could leave. Was Roany ever glad to see me! I watered and fed him, then rode him home to do chores and get supper.

Things look bad again. We're having such hot, windy weather the crops have already blown out and the pasture is going fast.

June 22, 1936, Monday

Arrowwood Lake is getting very low. Jim Lake dried up weeks ago, and dust is blowing out of it in clouds these days.

Last Wednesday Dad went to Fargo to consult a good lawyer about the condemnation of his land. Now that the acquisition men have most of the land needed for the refuge, they seem to think they can get Dad's for less than the terms of the option by condemning it. The government is insanely throwing away money on this refuge, yet cheating the landowners out of their land.

Since then Bell has shown up and talked to Dad and Grover about settling up. I think he really wants to, as having owners still here must be completely unacceptable to him. But why don't these government guys ever get together on any matter and do something?

This grazing deal is a mess. I've recorded the disastrous prairie fire Dowson started last fall. Grover raised hell with him until finally, this spring, Dowson replaced Grover's pasture by having the CCCs fence in government land equivalent to that of Grover's they burned.

Now Bell says the government does not own that land; it belongs to some insurance company. The company will want rent because Grover's cattle are eating off their hay land. Grover replied he can prove Dowson fenced it for him, so Dowson or the government can jolly well pay the rent.

A few days later I listened on the party line when the boss in Minot phoned Dowson to tell him a big shot of the Biological Survey was out in North Dakota from Washington, D.C, and would be at Arrowwood that afternoon. "Have all your crews working and have things slicked up pretty nice so he won't be hopping on your back."

That afternoon I rode up on Grover's land and swung the binoculars around. More work was being done on the Arrowwood Waterfowl Refuge in that one afternoon than had been done in the preceding year. CCC crews were busily working at headquarters and the tower, were moving a building, doing something at Jim Lake, and building fences. Trucks were scuttling back and forth. Dowson was certainly pretending to be accomplishing something.

The school superintendent at Sentinel Butte wrote that I was elected for the job, and please to let him know at once if I would accept it. I did. When Seth came that evening he was very upset and angry to learn that rather than being only fourteen miles from him and my family, I'd be three hundred miles away in those "Godforsaken Badlands." I confided to my diary:

GEE-EE-WHIZ! He's as bad as my family. I should always be right here. Fourteen hundred miles would be better, but three hundred miles from all of them will help. For a long time I've wanted to get out of here. Now is my chance. I'm taking it.

After Seth left I rode up on a high hill and looked over my Stony Brook country, deciding I will not miss it very much. After all the changes the government is making, it isn't home to me any more.

Then I rode to tell Grover about my job. He is pleased for me. As for himself, he is not going to the Badlands this fall and may never go. He says he intends to stay here as long as possible.

Bud, working at Carrington, was close enough to come home every Sunday in June. Ethel spent the month visiting schoolmates and making job applications wherever she was staying.

July 6, 1936, Monday
Last Tuesday evening Roy and Seth drove down to say that Carver, who was assistant manager at Lower Souris Refuge, had just walked in and showed Seth a letter from the Regional Director saying the two of them are to change places. No one had told Seth.

Bell and Dowson must have worked it. Bell never investigates for facts, and Dowson has been blaming Seth for things Dowson did before Seth came here. Also, Bell does not like it that Seth is not married and does not have the house furnished. Carver is married. Seth was upset, but it may be all for the best. He is not happy here.

Thursday the Sentinel Butte Superintendent sent me the contract and a letter saying he wondered if, in addition to the subjects mentioned when I was hired, I will not also teach typing and shorthand and take care of the library and Girl Scouts, as well as all dramatics in the high school. They are paying me $90.00 a month, instead of $85.00, and I guess he wants to be sure I earn it.

Seth came down that evening. When I told him about the contract, he demanded I not sign it, as he wants me to marry him in September. How does he know he wants to marry me? We've only known each other a few weeks. We'v gone to a couple of dances and about three movies. He does drop in here every time he can, so he has no illusions I'm a glamor girl. He sees me in work clothes, no makeup, and my hair blowing in the wind.

One of the many things I'm fed up with is men who get ideas of getting married! On our first date I plainly told him I would date him this summer and that was it—I would leave in the fall. He has a lot of good qualities but would be a difficult man to live with. When I told him marriage for us is impossible, he said I didn't realize how much thought he had been giving it. Doing me a big favor? I signed the contract.

The President of the school board in Courtenay has been very nice. He told me he didn't blame me for taking a better-paying job, but if I ever want another job in Courtenay, I need only come back.

Seth left for Lower Souris yesterday morning after coming down to say he will be back in September and we will be married. I told him there is no use even talking about it.

Bud has been transferred out to Bismarck.

It was 118° in the shade today. Some of my chicks died in spite of water and shade. At sunset Dad sent me to the southwest pasture to see if the calves had lived through the day. They had.

Bud was transferred to a survey gang at Hebron in the western part of the state. He was paid sixty dollars a month plus fifty dollars for living expenses. He felt he could save his salary and some of his living expense money to have a tidy sum for college by mid-September. I would get ninety dollars and pay thirty dollars for room and board. Some new clothes would be necessary from the first month's salary, but after that I could help him. Ethel did not yet have a job, but at least she was through school.

July 9, 1936, Thursday
It is still beastly hot. I went riding this afternoon and noticed they are still making walks at headquarters, a job the CCCs have been on since early May. Roy, the foreman in charge of the job, gets so disgusted, saying, "If they would leave me alone for four days, I would get done!"

Walks are to connect all the buildings at the Headquarters, which are presently a house, barn, big garage and machine shop, and an office. Dowson ordered walks made of cement. After one was done he decided that was too expensive and ordered them made of gravel. The graveled walks were no sooner finished than Dowson got orders they were to be made of stone. After they took up the gravel and made walks of small stones fitted together, some big shot from D.C. came along and had a fit over that, ordering them to use big rocks. So they took out the small rocks, and dug holes to fit big rocks in, leaving spaces for grass to grow between the rocks. The next big shot from D.C. who came along said there were not to be spaces between the rocks. So now the big rocks are being fitted closely together until *another big shot comes along who has a different idea.*

I told Roy this place is supposedly being developed for a breeding ground and place of refuge for the waterfowl, so I wondered why so much time and money was being spent on walks at Headquarters.

"You'll wonder about a lot more things than that!"

July 11, 1936, Saturday
This is the eighth day of terrible heat. Mama is just bedridden from it. Dad is at Commissioners' meeting. Al has all he can do to manage a bit of field work and take care of the horses. I've been tending the housework and poultry and helping Joe with the milk cows, calves, and hogs.

Yesterday was 110° with a hot wind blowing. Today is the same. I'm writing this lying on the living room floor, dripping sweat and watching the dirt drift in the windows and across the floor. I've dusted this whole house twice today and won't do it again.

Last night, when it cooled a bit, I rode out to see if the cattle were all right. When I got home at 9:30, Ethel and Ray were leaving for a dance. Ethel said Joe had given up and gone to bed without getting the milk cows in. It is still daylight this time of year until about 10:00. It took me until midnight to get those eleven cows home and milked.

This morning I had to do all the chores. The heat has just laid poor old Joe out. I set the bread very early this morning, hoping before it got too hot Ethel would get it in the oven while I did the outside work. But she left at 9:30 last night and hasn't come home yet, so I had to do the baking in the heat of the day. I'm just about laid out, too.

Well, writing this is not getting the churning done, and I'll have to do all the chores tonight.

In July, Dowson sent letters to Grandma, Grover, and Ted saying he was going to put firebreaks on their land. If they had any objections, they were to let him know at once. Grover wrote "Permission Refused" on all three letters, and I rode to Dowson's office. He wasn't there, so I gave them to his clerk, telling him Dowson's firebreaks were more disastrous than any accidental fire.

July 16, Thursday, 1936
It has stayed scorching hot.

Last evening Carver, the new refuge manager, came to see Dad. I visited with him half an hour before Dad got home. He seems a pleasant fellow. It is clear he doesn't like this refuge. Dad has him sized up as being very much under Dowson's thumb. He had come to see if, through Dad, he could borrow some county equipment. Needless to say, he didn't get it.

Today it cooled down to 104°, but with a hot wind. I rode to Grover's land at the lake. Grover is too busy, and wants me to keep an eye out for a firebreak or firebreak tractor.

Carver told me last evening that certain things could be done on land on which papers had been served. I suspected he had heard about Grover refusing permission for firebreaks and was hinting they could go ahead with them. He added they had no wish to borrow trouble, and I assured him it was a good idea not to do that.

Then he asked me how much of Grover's land had been taken. I told him to ask Grover. Actually, none of Grover's land has been taken. Carver and Dowson don't seem to know that. The Biological Survey doesn't seem to believe in letting the left hand know what the right hand is doing. I'm watching to see Dowson make the mistake of putting a firebreak plow on Grover's land. Finding no sign of it, I went home and fixed Dad a nice birthday supper.

Arrowwood Lake has developed a stench detectable for miles. A trench of seedlings right at the edge of the water in June is now 25 feet from it. McBride, the watermaster at Minot, told Seth the lake will not go dry this year. [It may not have; I do not remember. But I do recall that it was completely dry in the summer of 1937 and I rode Roany across the middle of the lake bed.]

The CCC boys are not supposed to indicate to anyone that conditions at the camp, that Utopia provided by the generous government, are not just wonderful. So when someone in town asked one of the boys about the water supply at camp, the answer was, "It's absolutely perfect. Couldn't be better. Twenty million tadpoles and lizards can't be wrong."

Well, it is 11:00 and I better get to bed. We're haying and have to get up at 4:00.

As the month wore on, Seth wrote frequently, telling how much he missed me and what he was doing. He expressed great dissatisfaction with the Lower Souris Refuge, the poor food at camp, and the lack of potable water. He had visited the other two refuges up near the Canadian border, Upper Souris and Des Lacs, and thought little of them, either. All the refuge managers were fighting with the camp superintendents.

July 22, 1936, Wednesday
Sunday evening Cap took me to a movie in Jamestown. He is still apologizing and explaining about not taking me to that dance last May, but I say skip it and let bygones by bygones.

Saturday I listened to a call on our party line which was a telegram from Bell to Carver telling him to be careful not to antagonize the insurance company, and saying Grover was instructed in June he was running cattle there at his own risk.

Bell was lying. Grover was not told that. He is pasturing land Dowson fenced for him to pasture, and Bell himself agreed the fence to the windmill should be built first.

In the evening I rode to tell Grover about the telegram. He laughed and laughed. "So they are not to antagonize the insurance company? Mr. Nielson, representing the agency, has been here to see me. He was already antagonized at those guys, and when I got through with him he was more so."

Nielson had told Grover the company didn't care about rent. They just wanted the government to pay for the land. The 1934 option has long since expired. Bell won't answer their letters. Nielson did suggest Grover take his cattle out and get Dowson to fence something else for him.

"I won't. I've been scrapping with Dowson ever since last fall to get enough pasture for my cattle. I've got it, and I'm going to keep it. If you want to scrap with Dowson, there's the road to camp."

He wished Nielson luck in getting settlement but told him what the government had done to other landowners here. Neilson went right up in the air. Oh, he's antagonized, all right. So he went to Dowson, who passed the buck to Carver, who must have wired Bell. I heard the answer.

I feel rather sorry for Carver, who, as a newcomer, is unaware of all the dirty tricks these other bureaucrats have pulled and the lies they have told. If he has brains enough to talk to Grover, and brains enough to know Grover tells the truth, he'll get along. Otherwise he won't. It will be interesting to see what kind of man he is.

Grover asked what I would do in his place. I said just what he is doing—sit tight. I don't think the company will do a thing. They can't sue the federal government, but I hope they do something to give Dowson a black eye with that Bell he is always toadying to, or something to get Bell into trouble with his bosses in D.C.

Bell is trying to keep peace with everyone, no matter how many lies he has to tell to do it. Due to career ambitions he doesn't want to rock the boat or get anyone in D.C. questioning his management. But ever since Grandma's land was taken, Grover and the rest of us have been on the warpath. Some bureaucrat better do something soothing pretty soon.

July 29, 1936, Wednesday
Uncle Chris was here last week and asked me how many ducks there are at Arrowwood Lake. I estimated about 600.

"Then it is costing the government $3.00 per day per duck."

That rapidly drying lake is the only body of water left in this area. Hundreds of little ducks, hatched on the prairie, perished before they could reach water. Carver could have had the CCCs rescue most of them, but Carver does nothing about anything.

I heard Dowson talking to the Valley City nursery. He said there is only a foot and a half of water in what is left of the lake, and the Biological Survey has lost 140,000 seedlings this summer. I wonder why, in view of the prolonged drouth, they were ever ordered and what numbskull ordered them.

Sunday night I went to a movie with Cap.

Monday I washed and ironed in the morning and spent the afternoon helping the men round up the calves and vaccinate them for blackleg. I drove the calves back to pasture in the evening and then rode over to see Grover and Grandma.

Grover told me the CCCs have always quit work at 3:00 P.M. but lately have been working until 6:00. I told him they were not working longer hours, but have two shifts; half work in the morning and the other half in the afternoon. When he had seen the men working so late, he thought some bigshot from Washington must be coming.

One night Ted saw them digging rock out of a sidehill after six and remarked, "President Roosevelt himself must be coming."

The CCCs haven't finished a single project, not even the walks at Headquarters.

Seth wrote there is a chance he will be sent as manager to the Des Lacs Refuge in the northwest corner of the state. The Powers That Be have decided the present manager there will not do. Seth doesn't think much of it as a refuge, but doesn't think much of Lower Souris, either, the way it is being managed. He complains I don't write often enough or long enough letters. He probably never noticed I have a few things to do besides write to him.

Bud wrote he has been transferred to Glen Ullin, a small town east of Hebron.

August 1, 1936, Saturday

July has gone, and still no rain. This is the worst summer yet. The fields are nothing but grasshoppers and dried-up Russian thistle. The hills are burned to nothing but rocks and dry ground. The meadows have no grass except in former slough holes, and that has to be raked and stacked as soon as cut, or it blows away in these hot winds. There is one dust storm after another. It is the most disheartening situation I have seen yet. Livestock and humans are really suffering. I don't know how we keep going.

Seth continues to write pages and pages of complaints about living conditions and about his work. He bitterly reproaches me that I go out with anyone else. I went out with Cap years before Seth ever came here and may do so after he has gone back East. What is it to him?

The dirt quit blowing today, so I cleaned the house. What a mess! The same old business of scrubbing floors in all nine rooms, washing all the woodwork and windows, washing the bedding, curtains, and towels, taking all the rugs and sofa pillows out to beat the dust out of them, cleaning closets and cupboards, dusting all the books and furniture, washing the mirrors and every dish and cooking utensil. Cleaning up after dust storms has gone on year after year now. I'm getting awfully tired of it. The dust will probably blow again tomorrow.

Carver was down to see Dad about whom it would be advisable to rent hayland to and what could be done to prevent a recurrence of *the snow trouble of last year on the road north of us.*

Dad told him as far as he, as County Commissioner, is concerned, nothing will be done. The road was built by the county with the understanding the township would maintain it. The township officers, after seeing what the CCC trucks do to that road, flatly refuse to maintain it.

Dad said there is apt to be snow trouble again this year. The camp will have to cope with it. The township and county can't. This is a large county with only two snowplows and no money to buy more. Dad's district is one-fifth of the county, comprising twenty-four townships of six square miles each. So the CCC camp, in fact, this whole township, is entitled to only one-twenty-fourth of the work done by those plows in one-fifth of the county. The taxpaying farmers, in spite of anything Dowson says, are more entitled to the use of the equipment than the camp is. Dad told Carver that in view of all the money the government is pouring into trucks and Caterpillars the boys just wreck, it would seem sensible for the government to buy them a snowplow of some kind.

In early August, Ethel got a teaching job in a small town in the southeastern part of the state, and Grover went to Fargo to consult the same lawyer Dad did because papers had been served that the government was taking his land.

One evening I noted that Joe was leaning against the corral fence listening to a coyote singing up on the western hill.

"Dey say dis Logical Survey outfit is goin' to kill all de coyotes. Dey shouldn't do dat. A few coyotes don't hurt nottings und keep de gophers and rabbits down. All my life I listen to de coyotes in de hills. Sounds like home. Dey belong dere, else vy God put dem dere? Huh?"

"I don't know, Joe, and they sound like home to me, too. Only from here on out, God won't have much say about what lives on this range." I wrote, "To me, that lonely old man with his insight into the balance of nature, my grandmother snapping off her hearing aid in front of the land acquisition agent, and the defiant coyote up in the hills all stand for something we are losing. All three will soon be dead. One hopes their spirit carries on."

CHAPTER 10

Current of the Wind

By mid-August, 1936, we were feeding hay to the cattle because there was no grass left even along the roadside ditches. Livestock was being shipped out every day to prevent starvation, and it appeared that all the farmers who could get their hands on enough money to gas their old jalopies and leave were leaving North Dakota.

For the country as a whole the depression began in 1929, but for Dakota farmers, hit by low prices and high costs in the 1920s and the hailstorm of 1928, it began sooner. Drouth lasted for nine years in North Dakota and for seven years in the Great Plains states as a whole. Buffalo grass, which had held the soil in place, had been plowed up. Crops that supplanted it just withered and died. There was nothing to hold the soil against the everlasting winds. In the 1930s forty million acres of Great Plains soil simply blew away. Dust drifted on roads and along buildings and fences much like snowbanks.

I hate to remember the human and animal suffering. Prices were too low to make cattle worth shipping. On the other hand, there was no feed for them and no money to have feed shipped into the area. Water supplies became scarcer and scarcer. Farmers and ranchers hauled water many miles for their households and most valuable livestock. Other livestock, too weak to live long and not worth selling, were simply shot. Many cattle and horses, searching for feed and water, drifted until their strength was gone and died where they fell.

Weary farmers and ranchers, unable to buy feed or pay taxes, unable to save their blowing fields, struggled to save foundation herds of breeding stock and carried water to their gardens in hope of raising a few potatoes and cabbages to eat. Housewives fought a continual battle against dust, which was particularly irritating given the shortage of water.

Panaceas divised by the New Deal for relief, such as the Resettlement Administration, the Agricultural Adjustment Act, and abandonment of the gold standard, did nothing for the nerves of farmers and ranchers. Other relief was also inadequate. The Red Cross sent freight carloads of food into the Dust Bowl. A woman who lived at Wolf Point, Montana, during those years told of going to the railroad depot when she heard that a Red Cross freight car was due with fresh vegetables for people who had none and no money. She and her husband and six children were in that situation. Too many others were. Her familys' share of that whole load of vegetables amounted to one cabbage and three carrots.

In late August, Bud wrote from Glen Ullin asking how much help I would be able to give him at college. He had not been able to save as much money as he had hoped, but could keep his job until December. We knew Dad would not be able to help him at all. I told him to go back in September so he could graduate with his class. Surely with his part-time job in Fargo, his summer savings, and what I could send him after buying a few necessary clothes and paying the insurance premium, he could get through the year.

He wrote, "Sis, did I ever tell you about this here city of Glen Ullin? We live in a big-league hotel. There is a pitcher and a catcher in each room. The pitcher is always empty and the catcher is always full. The NPRR [Northern Pacific Railroad] is just 75 feet from the front door, and about ten trains go by in the day and twice as many at night. And boy, are the trains long! They are so long (the freight trains, I mean) that the engine is going 40 miles an hour before the caboose gets started. The passenger trains go through here so fast they are out of sight before the stop light at the crossing goes on. Oh, this is a real place."

Seth was transferred to manage the Des Lacs Refuge at

Kenmare in the northwestern corner of the state. He continued to write long letters and reproached me for not doing likewise. I merely grumbled in my diary, "He was around here enough to see I have lots to do besides write to him. It probably never dawned on him, though."

I received a letter from the superintendent at Sentinel Butte saying school would start September 7. The faculty would meet on Saturday, the fifth, at 2:00 P.M. He wanted to know if I could handle public speaking and journalism in addition to the Latin, typing, shorthand, dramatics, social science subjects, Girl Scouts, physical education, and the library.

Of course I could, but I thought something was fishy. The English and history teacher had left the previous spring. That was the job I had applied for. Fortunately, I was qualified for Latin, social science, and commercial subjects and was hired for those. I had agreed to take dramatics. But public speaking, dramatics, journalism, and the library were usually part of the English teacher's job. It seemed odd all that was being shoved on me.

Of the last few days at Stony Brook my diary says,

Sunday evening I went for a moonlight horseback ride—possibly my last in the Stony Brook country. I sat for a long time on a hill southeast of the lake looking over the area I once loved so much. Its beauty is gone. CCC roads penetrate coulees where only cattle, Roany, and I used to go. The river is spoiled with their dams. The camp and its activities are everywhere. Our old neighbors are all gone and their houses torn down. Now the landscape is blotted with that ugly and expensive Refuge Headquarters and even more ugly sprawling set of buildings housing the CCCs. This isn't home any more.

Aunt Nettie wrote asking me to spend the weekend in Medora. Lee will take me to the faculty meeting in Sentinel Butte Saturday afternoon and take me back there Sunday evening. She wants me to spend my weekends with them.

Thursday evening I rode to Grandma's to say goodbye. Aunt Evalyn is leaving for New York soon and wants me to visit her in Woodstock next summer. The practical nurse they had last spring will stay with Grandma this winter.

Dad took me to Jamestown early on the 4th as he had Commis-

sioners' meeting. I spent the day with Audrey and took the midnight
bus to Medora.

At the Rough Riders Hotel Saturday morning I met the architect for
the local CCC camp. Why are architects hired for CCC camps? All
they have are ugly barracks all alike. He asked me to go and see the
camp with him. I politely refused. I have seen enough of CCC camps.
That tickled Lee. He says the architect considers himself quite a lady
killer.

In the afternoon Lee took me to the faculty meeting, which did not
take long. The Superintendent had the schedule all made out. Back at
Medora I climbed the butte behind the hotel and watched the sunset.
From up there the Chateau de Mores was dwarfed in the majesty of
the buttes.

In the evening Lee and I went to the show and then to the Sunset
Cave clubroom. There was nothing much going on there, so I went to
bed early and never woke up until Sunday noon. That was the best
rest I can remember.

September 7, 1936, Monday
Lee brought me to Sentinel Butte last night. Ila, a nineteen-year-old
girl who teaches third and fourth grade, and I will share rooms and
will board at the Butte Hotel.

There are four high school teachers and less than fifty students,
most of them bussed in from the country. The English and history
teacher, Miss Anderson, had Ila's job last year. I don't know how she
got this high school job I wanted except that she must have some pull
with somebody. She is a silly, incompetent woman, I already know, and
so it is obvious why the Superintendent pushed off on me some of the
work the English teacher usually does.

Between classes and library I have a full schedule from 9:00 until
4:30. All the declamation, journalism, play practice, and such work is
done after 4:30. The teachers are expected to be at the schoolhouse
from 8:00 A.M. until 5:00 P.M.,—if extracurricular activities don't take
until 6:00 P.M., and sometimes from 7:00 until 9:00 or 9:30.

September 10, 1936, Thursday
It is time to tell about Sentinel Butte and my new life. This is a town
on the west edge of the Badlands, about 17 miles west of Medora and

ten miles east of the Montana line, It is on the main line of the Northern Pacific Railroad and on Highway #10, which is being rebuilt.

The town is on a level place between North Butte and Sentinel Butte. North Butte is not very big but has a fine view. Sentinel Butte, 2½ miles south of town, is the second highest point in North Dakota, 3,400 feet, and is three miles long and half a mile wide. Its name comes from the fact that General Custer posted sentinels there on his way to the Little Big Horn. I believe history records his troops were caught in a snowstorm here in May, 1876.

The population of this town is about 300. Most of the residences are north of the highway and the businesses south of it. There are three churches, Catholic, Lutheran, and Congregational. The people are very poor and the buildings shabby. The businesses are a grain elevator, lumber yard, post office, 2 pool halls, a bank, barber shop, hardware store, 3 grocery and general merchandise stores, drug store, depot, garage, filling stations, cafe, and the hotel, which also serves meals.

A two-story brick building houses the four grade school rooms downstairs and the high school upstairs. Most of the students seem to be above average. The Superintendent says there are no loafers or discipline problems. These kids know what they want. They and their parents sacrifice for their high school opportunities, which they are not inclined to waste.

Mr. and Mrs. Higby run the Butte Hotel, a big, ramshackle building unchanged from forty years ago, I suspect, except that the paint has peeled off. A gas furnace and little gas heaters heat the downstairs. Upstairs rooms used merely for sleeping have no heat. Since the teachers spend much time evenings and weekend in their rooms, they have small gas heaters to make the rooms livable.

Downstairs are the dining room, kitchen, and rooms for the Higbys and the help. Up the narrow stairs and ranged along both sides of a narrow hall are a number of very small bedrooms. A store manager, men of the road crew, and all the teachers except Miss Anderson, and the Superintendent, who is married, live in those rooms.

Ila and I got rooms #6 and #8, side by side and each opening only into the hall. With the Higby's permission we moved the bed out of #8 to use it as a living room while we both sleep in the bed in #6.

Our living room has orange walls stippled with white spots and a

floor painted gray. It is furnished with a broken-down daybed, a green
and white table, and two straight-backed chairs.

Our bedroom is painted purple with green spots stippled on. The
floor is orange, but fortunately there is little paint left on it. A few nails
pounded in a corner serve as closet space. The room is furnished with
a bed, dresser, rag rug, and a washstand which holds a big china
washbowl with brilliant red poppies painted on it and a pitcher
painted with pink daisies. The catcher is plain white. There isn't room
for both Ila and me in that room unless one of us is in bed.

Both rooms are unheated, so Ila and I had a small gas stove put in
room #8. We can get along without heat in the bedroom. When the
plumber installed the heater, I protested there is no room on it for a
teakettle.

"Why, may I ask, do you want to put a teakettle on this stove?"

"To heat water to wash our faces."

He looked at me pityingly. "Lady, you'll never get any hot water in
this hotel. You'll have to dryclean your faces."

Plumbing just isn't. By going down the back stairs and making a
forty-yard dash down the alley, we can reach the outhouse, often only
to find someone else got there first. When we want warm water to
wash our clothes or ourselves, we go to the well down the alley, pump
the required amount of water into a pail to carry to the hotel kitchen,
push a pan of hash aside on the coal range, heat the water, carry it
upstairs, and dump it in the red poppy washbowl.

The hotel is as noisy as a calf corral, what with everyone's radio
going and the road construction crews, who work day and night,
changing shifts. The food is monotonous, mostly fried meat, fried
potatoes, bread, butter, and pie. But the Higbys are kind, and the help
doesn't mind our wandering into the kitchen any old time for a cup of
coffee.

In those days young ladies were supposed to have escorts to
public functions, even for dances the school was sponsoring. Ila
and I soon discovered there were only three young men in town
eligible as escorts, and one, whom we called "Ossified Oswald,"
was not really eligible because he drank too much. That left Mark
and Jason. Jason I remember as a handsome lad whose conversation was a running stream of nonsense. His father having died

the year before, Jason had to quit the university to run his father's grocery store and help his mother raise eight younger children. He was Ila's escort that year. Mark, a few years older than Jason, worked to support himself and his widowed mother during the week at the Theodore Roosevelt Park being developed near Medora and on Saturday at Jason's store. Kind, considerate, and a lot of fun, he was my escort.

I liked life at Sentinel Butte. We teachers had to do a staggering amount of work, but we were used to it. The library had not had proper care or cataloging for years. The superintendent assigned two National Youth Association girls to help me thirty hours a week, evenings and Saturdays, so I finally got caught up there. The National Youth Association (NYA) was a government program that gave work to needy students.

We had time for fun, too, dancing, horseback riding, hiking, playing Monopoly some evenings, or we teachers sat around visiting as we did chores like mending clothes. I spent quite a bit of time at Medora with the Fergusons.

September 29, 1936, Tuesday

Lee stopped in Friday night wanting me to go to Beach with him, but I couldn't because I had to chaperon a school party. He picked me up on the way home. When we got to Medora we sat up talking until 2:00 A.M. There was whoopee in Medora all night.

At 4:00 A.M. some fellow who had signed up for room # 5 came in and found a girl sleeping in that room. Every other room was full. Lee says he came and made quite a fuss to Lee. If he hadn't, Lee would have offered half his bed. As it was, he went back to sleep and let the chappie fuss.

Of course, the girl should not have taken the room if it was signed for. The only room in the hotel with a lock is the bathroom. Unlike most hotels out here, the Rough Riders has a bathroom, but only one, for all the guests, family, and help. One better not lock that door for long. The other rooms, as at the Butte Hotel, have no locks. There is no register at the Butte Hotel. At Rough Riders, at night, a lighted lamp and a register are left in a corner of the dining room. Anyone who comes in late registers himself for any room with no name beside the room number and goes to bed.

Sometimes tourists get bent out of shape over doors that don't lock. However, people and their possessions are perfectly safe here.

One night that winter I was at Medora, intending to take the night bus back to Sentinel Butte, when a raging blizzard struck. The bus would be very late, if it came at all, so Lee told me to go to bed in no. 10. A certain truck driver always had that room on Friday nights, but, in view of the weather, would not get east of Glendive that night, or certainly not beyond Wibaux.

Long after midnight that driver got to Medora. He walked into no. 10 and saw me asleep there, so he went down the hall and shoved Lee over to the other side of his bed. When I came downstairs the next morning, I heard the driver telling the kitchen help, "I came up to my room last night and walked in and turned on the light. And here was this female voice saying, 'No, no, a thousand times no.' " Of course I hadn't said anything. A sound sleeper, I hadn't heard him come in.

Saturday I did a lot of hiking. The country is aglow with autumn colors. That night we had a party and again not much sleep. I got up early because two men were waiting for my bed.

Seth sent another long letter. The Carvers had been up in a truck to get a scraper from the warehouse at Des Lacs. I guess Carver and the Army officers must be convinced they better do something to clear their own roads this winter.

"As usual he wouldn't open up, but he said enough to make it quite clear that he is having rough sledding and not exactly enjoying things. Bell has been there just once—answers letters weeks late—shoots telegrams at him—in fact, things seem to be progressing exactly as before. He has no assistant, and did my building full of equipment make him jealous! No more land has been paid for."

He writes all the pros and cons of his Christmas plans to go home and full details about his bowling games. That is about all, except how much he loves and misses me.

October 6, 1936, Tuesday
Saturday I got up early to direct the NYA work in the library and then hiked with Ila and Jane to see the crew surfacing the highway. It was

fun to watch. Ila and I rode horseback all afternoon. In the evening we chaperoned a marshmallow roast. When it was over, Jason and Mark offered us a ride home. Then we decided to drive over to Beach, eight miles west of Sentinel Butte. We finally wound up at a barn dance somewhere south of Wibaux, Montana. We had a wonderful time.

Sunday Ila and I rode horseback again.

Lee came up to visit us last night.

Tonight was our evening to wash and press clothes. Then I went for a walk in the misty moonlight. Oh, it's wonderful to be out in the midst of these weirdly shaped buttes all alone at night when the moon is full and the coyotes serenading it.

Seth wrote acting like a jealous bear because I've gone out with someone else. I'm rather annoyed that he acts so possessive and will certainly let him know it—when I get around to answering his letter.

October 15, 1936, Thursday

Jason and Mark have decided to collaborate on a book while Ila and I do another. Theirs will be The Private Life of a Prune Peddler and ours will be The Private Life of a Schoolma'am.

Last Saturday, bless his ambitious heart, the Superintendent had a Community Play Day. We teachers had to help. It was cold and windy with dust blowing.

Ila and I attired ourselves in boots and breeches and ate all the odds and ends in the hotel for breakfast. Then we went to work supervising Play Day while the scoria, red earth of the Badlands, liberally plastered us.

The crowd was mostly kids and dogs. Any adult who didn't have to be out in such weather had sense enough to stay home. The activities were games, races, a greased pole, a greased pig, and then a football game in the afternoon. When we finally got home it took a lot of soap, hot water, and cold cream to get us merely reconditioned.

In the evening we went with Jason and Mark to a dance the school was sponsoring.

Sunday we caught up on sleep. Nothing happened yesterday except I wrote the first chapter of

The Private Life of a Schoolma'am

"Brrr-ing! Ding-a-ling."

I open one eye. That isn't our alarm but one down the hall. Another snooze.

"Brr-rr-ing!"

That is ours. Ila shuts it off, hops out of bed, and announces the room is colder than Greenland's icy mountains. After dressing and having toast and coffee, we arrive at the schoolhouse at 8:00. There are six-week exams to be made out. I start the shorthand test, constantly interrupted.

"Can I get excused from typing for the next two days so I can catch up on my shorthand? Or I won't be able to take the shorthand test."

"When do you expect to catch up on your typing to take the typing test?"

"Miss Anderson is going to excuse me in history so I can take typing that period the rest of the week."

"But I can't supervise typing that period."

"Miss Anderson said I could do it in the office."

"Then when are you going to catch up on your history?"

"Miss Anderson said that after the shorthand exam you could excuse me from shorthand class so I could catch up on history."

"This is getting too complicated for my feeble brain. Go clear it with the Superintendent."

I wrote twelve more word signs.

"Do you know where Miss Anderson is?"

"I haven't seen her this morning."

"Well, will you help me with this history report?"

"I'll try."

"Where is Miss Anderson?"

"I haven't seen her this morning."

"When you get through helping with that report, will you help me fill out my history workbook?"

The shorthand test is abandoned in despair.

9:00. The Superintendent makes announcements in assembly.

Typing class, with a chance to supervise that and make progress on the shorthand test.

Shorthand class. Give the test, announce a review of phrases for tomorrow, and answer a lot of questions.

During the next period run the library.

Lunch time. To the post office and no mail. Back to the schoolhouse to spend the rest of the noon hour making lesson plans for public speaking class.

"Is Miss Anderson back from lunch?"

"I don't think so."

"Then will you help me with this English?"

The bell rings. To public speaking class, where the lesson is a review of all we've studied about diacritical markings and pronunciation.

The bell rings. As I head for Latin class, the county recreational director corners me in the hall to tell me how to start a Girl Scout troop. I finally get it through his head that I started one in Courtenay and have already started one here. He tells me all the difficulties he is having with his Boy Scouts in Beach. Meanwhile my Latin class is having a fine time.

Arrive in Latin class in time to hear the translation and explain the vocative case.

The bell rings. Back to the library to check out books and help the English students with their reading lists.

4:00. Check in books, direct NYA girls, and give makeup tests.

5:00. Ila is through work and suggests we go downtown. No mail. We go to the hotel and wash off the day's layer of dust.

6:00. We go downstairs to supper, having first run to the store to purchase boxes of soap to wash all our dirty clothes in the red poppy washbowl. The other teachers are planning the same kind of entertainment for the evening.

6:30. We go upstairs and wash clothes, press clothes, mend clothes, wash our hair, and manicure our nails.

Then it is 11:00. Ila goes to bed. I start writing The Private Life of a Schoolma'am. Write this chapter and decide to write no more as the darned life isn't worth writing about anyway.

THE END

We got paid Tuesday. Our first month's pay was two weeks overdue, and we teachers have been living on credit. I can't buy any clothes out of this check. Mama wants money to get her glasses changed, and Bud wants any I can spare. His tuition, clothes, books, and first month's board and room cost him all he had saved all summer and he has not been able to get enough work this fall to keep him going.

Mama wrote the WPA men were building a dam until told the

Biological Survey has the water rights on the watersheds of the lake and river. So the WPA is busy undoing what it has done.

She writes, "200 WPA workers are being taken off the road work and put on the game refuge to help those poor hard-working CCCs. Some say they are fencing, others think they are rip-rapping islands. One man said he heard they are building muskrat houses. Anyway, the road program has been shot to pieces."

October 22, 1936, Tuesday
Last Friday morning Jane, the only teacher besides the Superintendent who owns a car, took us women teachers to Dickinson to the Teachers' Convention. It was a bore, and I am broke again.

Seth writes that he is going to send me a radio.

October 30, 1936, Friday
Last Friday night Mark and I went to a dance here. Lee came up for it and asked me to go back to Medora with him and go on political trips with him Saturday. By the time we got to Medora there were no empty rooms at the hotel, so I went down and bunked with the hashers.

Aunt Nettie says the Count de Vellombrosa has given the Chateau de Morés, which his father built in the early 1880s in Medora, to the State Historical Society.

According to stories I have heard and read, the Marquis de Morés was a Frenchman who married Medora von Hoffman, daughter of Baron von Hoffman, a New York banker. He came out here and established the town of Medora, built a big house, the Chateau de Morés, on a bluff above the river southwest of town, and built a packing plant. His plan was to process beef here and send it East in refrigerator cars instead of shipping beef on the hoof. The plant burned down many years ago, but the chimney still stands, looming high on the west edge of town.

The Marquis had other business adventures out here on which he lost money, but is said to have lost the most in the packing plant business. He was cheated by being sold the same cattle twice. Most of his sheep died. Meat packers farther east considered him a threat who must be put out of business and called upon Wall Street to ruin him. Railroads held up his beef shipments.

Within a few years, having lost about one and one-half million dollars, much of it belonging to his father-in-law, who refused to stake him any further, the Marquis and his family went back to France.

His son, Louis de Vellombrosa, has recently visited here and has arranged to give the Chateau to the State Historical Society. The caretaker, who shows tourists through the house for a small fee, points out that the furniture, rugs, dishes, linens, and even magazines remain just as the family left them in the 1880s. I have detected a jarring note. The caretaker is apt to leave in full view of the tourists a hideous dime-store ashtray in the shape of a human skull.

Lee and I had lots of fun Saturday on a campaign trip among the Bohemians and Ukrainians north of Belfield, through some of the people don't speak English, so we couldn't converse with them. Many of the houses are sod huts. The frame houses are painted in fantastic colors. A number of places have everything under one roof—the house, barn, chicken coop, and hog pen—a bit odoriferous, but handy in winter. Up at Snow we saw a beautiful Russian church.

At Fairfield we visited Mary Hecker, who went to high school in Medora. The Hecker place is the town of Fairfield. It is a large building in which the Heckers run a store and post office and live in the back. After a nice visit and supper there, we followed miles of goshawful road to Lillibridges, where there was a church bazaar and endless auction.

Monday there was a letter from Seth saying he misses me terribly and wonders if he can see me at Thanksgiving. I doubt it because coaching a play will be taking all my spare time.

Tuesday night Mark and I went to Beach to a movie, The Trail of the Lonesome Pine, in technicolor. It was beautiful. Now we not only have talking pictures, but in color instead of black and white. Movies are becoming more interesting all the time.

November 3, 1936, Tuesday
This is election day. When the tumult dies down, what will we do for excitement?

Friday night after school I went hiking alone until dark, and later to a dance with Mark.

Saturday Ila and I took the morning bus to Medora and went to an auction sale, where I had a happy reunion with old Ben Bird. He said he had surely hoped I'd get out here last summer and had kept horses up for Laura and me and picked a place for us to camp. I told him I'd have loved it but was needed at home all summer. Next time I get to Medora I'll take riding clothes, and he and I will go riding.

There is no problem borrowing a saddle horse out here, but I miss Roany and want to get him here. Dad doesn't use him much, preferring a bigger horse, and, after our place is gone, will have no place to put him. Here he could be boarded very cheaply. The problem is the money to truck him out here.

November 5, 1936, Thursday

Election was a landslide for Roosevelt. Langer is again governor of North Dakota.

I am diagramming scenes and getting things lined up for the senior play.

Seth wrote telling all he is doing and sounding very lonesome. He says again he is going to get me a radio. I should write to him but haven't money to buy a stamp. Again we teachers have not been paid. From my only check so far I sent money to Bud and Mama, went to the convention, bought a round-trip bus ticket to Medora last Saturday, and am flat broke.

We teachers can't help laughing over the reason we did not get our October pay. The president of the school board is angry because he was not re-elected county commissioner and refuses to sign our warrants. There is no reason to take his pique out on the teachers. We do not have residency and did not vote.

Bud writes he is getting along fine in school but will need more money before Christmas. Dad has none to send him, and Ethel says she doesn't either.

December 1, 1936, Tuesday

Six-week exams and play practice have been keeping me busy. We finally got our October pay when the president of the school board resigned. Saturday Ila and I took the bus to Beach and bought clothes. Except for shoes I got everything I needed, even a hat. I can get along a little while without new shoes and am waiting to see how much money Bud will need this month. Perhaps the hat wasn't really necessary. These days many young women just wear scarves, called "babushkas," over their heads. But teachers are expected to dress in a conventional and conservative way.

There has just been another letter, pages and pages long, from Seth. He gives a detailed account of the time he and his patrolman spent trying to catch a supposed poultry thief. I don't know why he doesn't leave that sort of thing to the sheriff. It turned out the poultry wasn't stolen anyway. He also wrote pages and pages on all the details of his bowling games.

He still claims the radio is coming; he is just testing models to be sure he gets one that is satisfactory. It is sweet of him to get me a radio, but all he has done for more than two months is write about it!

Soon I was rejoicing in my diary that I had bought no more clothes than absolutely necessary because Bud needed all the money I had left, and it took my last stamp to mail it to him. I told him there was no promise of when more would be available. We teachers had not been paid for November because the school district was completely broke. We had borrowed money from the bank to pay room and board for November. The banker said he would lend us no more until he knew whether we would be paid.

We Sentinel Butte teachers apparently were not worried. We were promised half our November pay before Christmas, and then the district would float a bond so that we would eventually get our money. Of course, with the bank loan and room and board to pay, we would have a lean Christmas. But we were used to lean Christmases.

Bud wrote that he was already in debt and might be faced with the expenses of enrolling for another semester before I would get my back pay. The only possible way I could get any money before the bond was floated would be to sell Roany. He was still a young horse and a good one who would bring a fair price from someone needing such an animal and able to afford him.

Neither Bud nor I could bear the thought of having Roany sold. Bud would just "run his face" (our term for charge accounts) and we would pray the bond would be floated in time for his second-semester expenses. It was.

December 16, 1936, Wednesday

The Senior play went off well, and the kids presented me a lovely bouquet of roses for coaching it.

Our half-month's pay for November came today.

Seth wrote last week fretting about not hearing from me. Well, I kept in touch with Mama and Bud with some penny postcards I had on hand. That proper New Englander would have been offended by a penny postcard. Of course I know he would gladly have sent me some stamps if he had known I had no money to buy any, but I didn't tell him.

Monday the radio came—a five-tube Philco—with a sweet card. He got his leave. I doubt if he will come back.

CHAPTER 11

Drifting with the Wind

January 2, 1937, Saturday

A new year has come. I'm writing this in bed in the Butte Hotel. And I am remembering that a year ago I was welcoming the year 1936 with high hopes. After all that happened in 1936, I won't be silly enough to welcome 1937 with high hopes for better times. However, I can say again, as I said a year ago, we've made it so far.

My diary got left back in the middle of December. We somehow survived the school Christmas program December 18, and some of the teachers left on the midnight bus that night.

Before I left for Jamestown, Mark told me he is going to persuade me to marry him if it takes the rest of his life. Well, that's what it would take. He's a fine man of whom I'm truly fond, but I don't want to get married. Also, he and I would always be on a collision course due to differing religious beliefs.

And what in the billy-blue-blazes would we live on? He supports his widowed mother, a lovely woman he adores. They own a cute little home, but only a four-room one, in the northeast part of town. Even Mark admits he could not expect a wife to move in there, too, and he could not support two households. If I should marry, I would lose my job immediately. Anyway, I don't want to get married, and that is that. A married woman loses all independence and any chance at a career of her own.

Bud met me at the bus in Jamestown, and we had a good visit all the way home. Mama looks well. Roany is fat and sassy. I was very busy before Christmas with baking and cleaning, but rode him a couple of times—enough to decide the Stony Brook country is surely spoiled. The CCCs have put in so many new fences one can't ride the old trails.

Ethel came up for Christmas dinner with her new boy friend who works in the town where she teaches. They are already engaged to be married, but I don't know how soon.

In 1937 the folks were still fighting about payment for the land. Dad's option would have paid him more than twenty-two dollars an acre. After all the other land was bought by hook or by crook, the government condemned our family's land, planning to pay Dad eighteen dollars an acre and Grover fifteen dollars. The lawyer finally got each of them two dollars more per acre and got Grandma twenty-eight dollars. He felt there was no use taking it to court because land prices were so low they were not apt to do better. Dad had permission to move one building. When he moved, he took the garage. Grandma got life tenancy, but only of the farmstead buildings and a little strip of land down to the river. Ted's health forbade his staying in that climate in winter, so he spent the winters with his sister Helen in Tulsa. Grover, of course, had to stay with Grandma, who could not be uprooted at her age. He rented land south of the place for pasture. The government rented him land for crops. That could keep him from starvation while awaiting payment. Mama and Dad also had to stay put until they were paid.

January of 1937, for me, was filled with school work, dances, Monopoly games, rabbit hunting with Mark and Jason, and arguing with Oswald. Mrs. Higby said she could not get any work done when Oswald and I were in the dining room at the same time because we would start arguing about anything, and she thought it funny to hear us try to top each other.

A pretty blonde named Adeline came to Medora as home agent for Farm Security in Billings and Golden Valley Counties. Lee fell in love with her.

I had changed direction on what to do with my life after the game refuge took over the Stony Brook country, but I had found something else, as illustrated by the following quotation from my diary.

George S., a local rancher, and I went horseback riding to take snapshots of the scenery. He told me Mrs. Smith is quite concerned about my future and what I'll do with my life. "She says you have too much beauty and personality to waste your life out here, and darned if I don't think she is right!"

I told him he and Mrs. Smith are very flattering, but I'm happy here and I like my job. Sure, once I hoped for a worthwhile life in the Stony Brook country. That is out. Sure, here I'm working like a dog for $90 a month, and the pay always late. But better times will come here. Meanwhile, I honestly feel I'm some help and encouragement to these kids. Almost all of them are very worthwhile young people having a struggle to get a high school education and facing a worse struggle to get college degrees. If I can inspire them to keep on struggling, some of them will be successful.

And, in the future, I don't intend to make my so-called living just as a teacher. Someday I'll be getting more pay and be able to keep it. I will have money to invest in livestock on shares. When livestock prices come back, and if land doesn't go too high at that time, I have my eye on a couple of good real estate investments.

Seth wrote in detail of his trip home, even what bus he took between trains. He went to Cape Cod for the Audubon Christmas count and told what they did each hour of the day and what birds they saw. He says he is going back to the Des Lacs Refuge. That puzzles me because he has never been happy in Dakota. It seems best he stay with his own kind of people. I guess he isn't happy there, either.

January 26, 1937, Tuesday

I spent the weekend down in Medora. Sunday was a great-granddaddy of a blizzard. The 3:00 P.M. train never got to Medora until midnight. By 1:00 A.M. it got me the seventeen miles to Sentinel Butte. The Butte Hotel was cold, there having been no heat since the gas went off Saturday night. It was twenty below outside and not much warmer inside. Wearing most of our clothes, Ila and I went to bed about 2:00 A.M. We just got warm enough to go to sleep when

Crack Higby came at 3:00 A.M. to put kerosene stoves in the dining room and made so much noise he woke us up.

Thinking what a finishing touch it would be if the hotel caught fire from those open stoves, we lay there and argued over what to try to save, who would crawl under the bed to get the fire escape rope, and who should try to open the window so we could slide down the rope to safety.

We sleepy teachers started the second semester in a bad mood. A letter from Seth did not improve my temper because, despite the fact I refused last summer, he seems to take it for granted he can persuade me to marry him. I fired off a letter making it clear I am not going to.

February 11, 1937, Thursday
The weather has been very bad. Ila and I went to Beach last weekend and had a good time.

Bud wrote thanking me for the money to pay his debts and enroll for second quarter, but wants more. If I can't help, he will be unable to enroll in spring quarter next month. No need to worry. I'll have two more pay checks by that time.

Seth wrote acting horrified that I called him selfish and domineering and then admitting that he is. He begged me to be his friend and keep on writing. I will probably write—when I get around to it. With the oratory contests and declamations to top everything else, I work all day and all evening.

February was a busy month and March even busier. The superintendent seemed please with what I had done in the declamation and oratory contests as well as directing journalism and plays. He hinted that he knew I was doing much of Miss Anderson's work, too.

In March a flu epidemic hit town. Within four weeks everyone had been sick at one time or another. Several people, including Mark's mother, died. It was a shock. She hadn't seemed to be very ill, then suddenly was gone.

In April the main events were putting on the junior play and getting notice that all the teachers but Miss Anderson were reelected. I felt sure sometime before school started in the fall the superintendent would get someone to replace me so that I could have English and history.

May 6, 1937, Thursday

We are busy working on the Junior-Senior Prom this week.

I've had a wonderful stroke of luck. The woman who runs the curio and gift shop in Medora has offered me a job for the summer. She has little business except in June, July, and August, when the tourists come through here. Then she runs the shop from 8:00 A.M. until 9:00 P.M. seven days a week, but feels too old and unwell to do that any more. She says she is impressed with my knowledge of the history and geography of this area and feels I could cope with the questions the tourists ask. Both of us would not be needed in the shop at the same time very often, so I would have a fair amount of free time. She wants me there when she takes an afternoon nap, when she is busy elsewhere, and in the evenings so she can go to bed early.

She says she can't possibly pay more than eight dollars a week, but there is a room in back where I can sleep. She will give me board, too, if I'll give her a hand with cooking, cleaning, laundry, and her garden. She is so apologetic about all that work for room and board and eight dollars a week that it amuses me. Working in the shop, plus housework for the two of us, is a drop in the bucket to all the work I've been doing for nothing every summer for years. Her garden is a postage stamp compared to what I've had to look after!

That money will enable me to have Roany trucked out here and I can save more than enough to have him boarded next winter. The pay will be pure velvet except that, having spent every summer for years in overalls doing ranch work, I have few summer clothes. I suggested that for very little money I can buy material to make old-fashioned square dance dresses and hire the filling station manager's wife to sew them for me. The shop owner fell right in with that idea, saying I'd look beautiful in clothes like that and make a big hit with the tourists.

This is going to be a fun summer. I can scarcely wait!

May 25, 1937, Tuesday

This is the last week of school in a year that has slipped away fast.

Last weekend Mark and I went to a picnic at The Cedars. He is lonesome since his mother died and still urging marriage. He has his little house and can support a wife now. He says if we wait one more year and save as much as possible, we would have a good start. He is a wonderful guy, but I don't want to get married. A married woman has no independence at all.

Speaking of marriage—Oswald, who is leaving for the coast soon, asked me to marry him. I was temporarily speechless. All we've ever seen of each other is dancing at every dance we have both attended and arguing all the time in the hotel dining room. He has mentioned marriage a couple of times at dances, but I paid no heed, knowing he would have forgotten it when he sobered up. This time he was sober.

Upon recovering my speech, I reminded him we scarcely know each other and never do anything but argue. "I don't know what has gotten into you, Oswald. You know you don't want to marry me."

"You're damned right I don't want to marry you! But you are a mid-Victorian prude no man can have without a marriage license. You are also a witty, strong-minded, argumentative female. Now that I've gotten used to you, I don't want to get along without you. So marry me, we'll go to the coast, and I'll show you a good time."

I told him within six months we would be divorced or one of us on trial for murder.

He is really a likable guy. Life as a newspaperman in Los Angeles made him totally unsuited for running a store in Sentinel Butte, North Dakota. No wonder he hits the bottle. I hope he finds his niche in life.

Seth wrote about ten days ago wanting to spend Memorial Day weekend at Medora. He might as well. He has bought a car now and can drive down here. He's considering throwing up his job and going back East.

Well, he can probably find a job there in the field of wildlife conservation. He really doesn't fit in here, and he misses bird clubs and squash games (whatever they are).

June 4, 1937, Friday
Seth came down to the Badlands on Memorial Day weekend, but the visit was not a success. He does not like the Badlands at all. We quarreled when I refused again to marry him and told him I am going to stay out here. He was so angry I said we better say goodbye. Then he was very contrite, saying he really loves me, can't bear for me to go out of his life, and begged me at least to go on writing to him. He

has phoned every night since, begging me to write. I'll do that sometime when I have time.

This is being written on a bus taking me back to Stony Brook, where I had hoped never to go again, and I feel very blue about it. Just as it seemed I was set up in a good job for a nice summer, a letter from Mama yesterday told me to come home as she and Dad need me.

Bud has a chance to work for the Highway Department at a better salary than ever before, expense money, and a chance to work seven days a week most weeks. He can't turn it down. He will probably make enough to see him through his last year at college.

Ethel isn't feeling well and has gone to Rochester for a checkup and a visit with the Johnson girls.

The government still has not paid for the land, so the folks have to stay there and eke out a living as best they can until payment comes. They are keeping poor old Joe as choreboy, but his rheumatism is so bad he is really not of much use. Dad's hip is bothering him so much he can't ride horseback any more, and Mama isn't able to be on her feet enough to manage the work with poultry, garden, and house.

I feel trapped in the same round all over again. Ethel never contributed a cent all year, so all I could spare, including almost all my last pay check, went to Mama and Bud. I have scarcely enough money for bus fare home—to just an everlasting round of work in the Stony Brook country that has been ruined.

This is a round that will go on forever. At least it will go on until my youth is gone. Somehow, I've got to get out!!

This, written June 4, 1937, is where the diary ends. I never wrote in it again.

The Dust Settles

I left my beloved Badlands in 1937. Twenty-five years passed before I could have gone back there to live. By that time everyone I had known there had died or moved away. Sentinel Butte had become practically a ghost town.

The Fergusons sold the Rough Riders Hotel at Medora in 1941 and moved to California. Lee and Adeline had married and moved to Ypsilanti, North Dakota, where they still reside after retiring from running a store and locker plant for many years.

A wealthy man bought the dying town of Medora, bypassed by the interstate highway, and made it the tourist mecca it is today. He restored the Rough Riders Hotel, the Ferris store, and various other historic buildings. Tourism has added a museum, motels and restaurants, art galleries, and souvenir shops. The Historical Society still maintains the Chateau de Morés.

Going back almost half a century in memory, it was in 1938, the first time in many years there had been enough moisture to raise a crop, that the government finally paid Dad for his land. He and Mama bought an old house and seven lots of land on the south edge of Kensal for fifteen hundred dollars. They rewired, repainted, and repaired the house and landscaped the grounds. Dad always missed the ranch, but he kept busy with a big garden and fixing up his new home. He was active in church, civic, county, and community affairs, and served on various volunteer boards during World War II.

Time, as always, wrought its changes. When Dad got his money, he at last discarded the Model-T Ford that had served us so many years and bought a new Ford sedan, which must have cost six or seven hundred dollars in those days. Joe was dead. Al still worked for Dad and, when that job was gone, went to work for Grover and spent his summers there until his death in 1963. Dad gave Bud's Model-A Ford to Al, who was still driving it in 1952. I don't know how long it lasted him after that.

When I could no longer keep Roany, I gave him to Grover. That horse lived to a good old age on Grover's ranch.

Even before the folks left the farm, I married Seth in spite of my rebellion against the social dictum of the time and place that the only career for a woman was marriage and a confining life of housework and raising children. Widows and single girls who had to support themselves might find work as store clerks, telephone operators, or, if lucky enough to have the education, as nurses, stenographers, or teachers. A married woman was not hired for those scarce jobs because she had a husband to support her. Even in the most unhapppy marriages divorce was almost unthinkable. A wife was expected to try in all ways to please her husband and to champion his actions and opinions regardless of what she really thought of them. Many women, such as my Aunt Nona, must have led lives of secret rebellion and frustration.

When I married, it seemed the only future after I had thrown away my job in the Badlands to go home and help the folks. By the time they no longer needed my help, all the teaching jobs were taken for that year. It would probably be at least a year before I could get one. Meanwhile, with no money, I would be dependent upon Dad for support in a purposeless life.

Seth declared he loved me and needed me in his career of wildlife management. He was honest and hard-working like my father. I thought I saw other characteristics of my father in him, only to learn later that the young man from luxurious surround-ings in a New England city and the old man who had grown up on the changing frontier could never have the same viewpoint and values.

When Seth and I had conflicting viewpoints, it helped me to remember how different our backgrounds were. The first time Seth and I visited his parents, his mother showed me where she wanted to put a mirror above a certain table in the entry hall, but complained there was no room. Above that table hung a large black and white print of silhouettes of the signers of the Declaration of Independence. Each silhouette was numbered, and at corresponding numbers below the picture the names were printed. I suggested she would have room for the mirror if she moved the picture elsewhere.

"My dear," she protested, "I could not move that picture! It has *always* hung there."

After several years at the Des Lacs Refuge, Seth was transferred to develop a new refuge in Oklahoma. By 1943, when he was called into the army, we had two children, a son and a daughter. After the war Seth returned to wildlife management, although he eventually left it to work as a research biologist in the East, where we remained until his death.

What was happening in North Dakota after we left?

In 1942 Ethel married a teacher from another state and left North Dakota permanently. Grandma died in that same year. Soon after, Grover married the beautiful, capable nurse he had met during Grandma's last illness. They rented the old homestead from the government until 1950, when Grover, Jr., reached school age, then moved closer to school to the farm Grover had bought at a tax sale in 1940. By that time they had remodeled the house there, planted shelterbelts of trees which are now towering groves, and added a number of buildings. Many years later Grover spoke to me of the years he had lost when the government took, at a fraction of its value, everything he had spent his youth working for.

On the other hand, God has given him far more than the number of years normally allotted to man, and health to get up and go to work at five o'clock in the morning as he has always done. The rundown farms he bought at tax sales more than forty years ago, augmented by land he and his son, Bill, have purchased since, are noted for their beauty, good planning, and good management. His place has been pictured in many publications, including *National Geographic* (July, 1976).

He has seen one son become a successful engineer, while the other is a partner on the farm. He has seen his wife, sons, daughter-in-law, and grandchildren take, as he has done, an active part in church, school, and community affairs. Looking back through the years, I believe Grover won out.

Dad lived to see and enjoy Grover's sons, but not to see them grow up. His heart suddenly stopped in the fall of 1948. Reminiscing, Grover said, "He always seemed as permanent as the Jim River hills." We all felt that way. It was not until after his death that I knew how much Dad had meant beyond our family. People came for hundreds of miles to his funeral.

Mama outlived Dad by fourteen years.

Bud graduated as a civil engineer in 1938 but could get no job except working on the highway as he had for several summers.

Seth and I picked him up at his job one day and took him to the county fair with us. As we entered the fairgrounds an acquaintance called, "Hi, Bud, I thought I saw you out on the highway job a little while ago."

"Maybe you did. What was I doing?"

"Not a thing."

"Yep, that was me."

Bud told us he and his college pals, Mike, Dale, and Tex, were enlisting in the Marine Corps.

"Civil engineers are a dime a dozen these days—no jobs. We can go into the Corps as second lieutenants, at $2,400 a year on a seven-year enlistment. After the first three years we go overseas and see the world. We have already passed our exams. There are only 40,000 men in the Marine Corps—hand-picked men. You people may touch me lightly—a beautiful hunk of man, one hundred percent perfect mentally, morally, and physically."

"One hundred percent sap," said Seth. "Don't you guys know there is another war brewing?"

"Sure, and the Marines will see all the excitement and get all the glory."

So Mike, Dale, Tex, and Bud joined the Marines in 1938, eager to see the world and the next war. The war ended quickly for Tex at Pearl Harbor. Dale starved to death in a Japanese prison camp. Mike survived the war after harrowing experiences related in a book called *The Dyess Story*.

One wintry Oklahoma day in 1946 I answered the doorbell and stared without recognition at a haggard man on the doorstep. "Sis!" he said, "you were such a pretty girl! In eight years you have aged twenty." In bed that night I cried a long time, not just for him, but for all the boys whose lives were scarred or ended by the war.

Bud went into civil engineering after his discharge from the Marine Corps and worked, in the United States and abroad, for topnotch firms, but never again found fulfillment and excitement in his work or personal life. One sunny July day he put a bullet through his head.

At Bud's funeral I sat dry-eyed and without hearing the service. I was back in 1931, seeing a tired boy riding one wornout horse and leading another, hearing him sing "The Great Roundup" as they plodded across the prairie.

I thought of the spirits in that funeral parlor: our great-grandfather, the straitlaced man who spent his life mining and guiding wagon trains on the frontier and devoted his money to the vision of a better life for his son; our talented grandfather slaving at work he was unfitted for and trying on a frontier homestead to win a better life for his children; our spirited, stout-hearted grandmother living her life according to her ideals until nearly eighty-five years old; my father, in his endless struggle against great odds, helping make his father's dream come true, and then losing his own high hopes of building up a ranch for Bud and the son Bud never had.

In 1983 I revisited North Dakota. The winters are still cold and long in the Stony Brook country. As Grover's son, Bill, remarked on a 23°-below-zero morning, "This kind of weather keeps the riff-raff out." The wind still blows in North Dakota, but is not blowing much dust. Fields have rows of shelterbelt trees, many of them evergreens, planted diagonally to break the wind. By cultivating on the contour, controlled grazing, and stubble mulching, erosion is controlled to a large extent.

The Missouri River Diversion Project, for which surveys were started in 1929, has not been finished and may never be, due to continuing opposition to it.

The small Arrowwood Refuge is still there, although preservation of wildlife does not appear to be its primary purpose. Hunting and many other activities are now permitted on it. The buildings, which, to our horror, cost $39,000 in the 1930s, have been razed and more buildings erected at even greater expense. The new office alone cost $324,000.

The towns I had known intimately are vastly changed. After World War II, improved automobiles and roads drew farm trade to the bigger towns. Jamestown has nearly tripled in size from the town I remembered. Penney's store is still there, but in a new shopping mall and without the fascinating little canisters on wires. Some small towns, such as Edmunds, have died completely. All the people I had known in Courtenay are dead or have moved away. Even the school is gone. Kensal and Pingree have fewer residents and businesses but have fine new consolidated schools and active churches.

Though all the buildings and fences in my old Stony Brook neighborhood had been destroyed between forty and fifty years earlier, Dad's shelterbelt trees are still there, and Grandma's apple and crabapple trees, one hundred years old, still bloom in a mass of undergrowth.

As for the farms of North Dakota—the good years we had awaited through dreary years came back, starting with the return of rainfall of 1938. In most years since, there has been enough moisture. World War II brought increased demand and prices for farm commodities. Farmers were able to pay their debts and buy more land and machinery to make their operations more efficient.

After the war came rural electrification. Running water and electricity now make farm homes as convenient as city homes. Better roads and automotive equipment ended the rural schools and led to well-equipped and well-staffed consolidated schools. The Farmers Union grew stronger and has more cooperatives.

Shipping points are now closer since the construction of the St. Lawrence Seaway.

There are more beef cattle on the farms now, and fewer hogs, sheep, chickens, and turkeys. Rust-resistant strains of grain have been developed. A new crop, sunflowers, more drouth-resistant than wheat, is partially supplanting wheat as the main crop.

The saddle horse or team and bobsled for all-terrain, all-weather transportation have been replaced by the four-wheel-drive pickup, the motorcycle, and the snowmobile. Huge trucks, instead of plodding six-horse teams with wagons, haul the grain.

Today a big machine cuts hay and runs it through a conditioner, leaving it in a swath. From the swath it is baled in 1,000- to 1,200-pound bales which shed rainwater. If left in the field, they are lined up end to end in multiples of four. A bale carrier loads and hauls four of these bales at a time. The carrier is pulled by tractor to a feeding lot, where one bale will feed twenty-five to thirty head of cattle—quite a contrast to hauling by team and hayrack the loose hay we had so laboriously cut, raked, and stacked.

Gone is the horse-drawn binder cutting a swath ten feet wide. The combine now cuts a swath twenty-two feet wide and threshes the grain as it goes. With a team of horses and a two-row cultivator, we used to cultivate 10 to 15 acres a day. Twelve-row cultivators, rapidly drawn by tractors, can cover 150 to 200 acres per day, and the tractors do not have to be rested on a hot afternoon for fear of killing them.

We used to seed 20 acres of grain a day with an eleven-foot drill pulled by horses. Now thirty-foot drills can seed 200 acres per day, and eight-row planters seed 150 acres of sunflowers. These machines are pulled by huge tractors with cabs protecting the driver from sun, wind, and cold. The newest and biggest tractors, which can cost as much as $176,000, are partially controlled by computers that give the driver constant information on how the machine is functioning. Even on the cheaper models, such as $70,000 ones, the cabs are equipped with a heater, air conditioning, radio, AM-FM stereo with eight-track tapes, and a CB for instant communication with home, neighbors, and business places. For convenience and efficiency, the CB beats the farmer's wife signaling him with a white dishtowel if he were in sight, or "putting a kid on a horse" if out of sight.

The 1983 wheat price of three dollars and sixty cents a bushel makes the thirty-two-cents-a-bushel wheat of the 1930s seem incredible. But by 1983 it cost sixty dollars per acre to produce wheat, and the farmer needed four dollars a bushel to make a profit. Cattle prices had changed, too, from one cent a pound for canners to thirty-two cents, and from four cents for steers to sixty cents. Calves such as those the government bought for four dollars apiece in the 1930s brought three hundred to three hundred and fifty dollars in the fall of 1983.

Land comparable to what the government bought in the 1930s to incorporate into the refuge, paying as little as ten dollars an acre, was selling in 1983 for from three hundred to nearly six hundred dollars an acre.

It is a joy to see how much easier life on farms and ranches is compared to the life we lived fifty years ago. The term "Dust Bowl days" means little now to young people, and even many people who lived through those days seem to have forgotten. After all, they may believe, it is a period of history that can never recur and is best forgotten.

Yet, as I looked around North Dakota and other Great Plains states, I thought I saw that some of the mistakes of farmers, bankers, and the government in the boom days early in this century are being repeated.

Rudyard Kipling's words, written in 1897, haunt me:

Lord God of Hosts, be with us yet,
Lest we forget—lest we forget.